WOMEN WHO LED NATIONS

PROFILES

Amazing Archaeologists and Their Finds
America's Most Influential First Ladies
America's Third-Party Presidential Candidates
Black Abolitionists and Freedom Fighters
Black Civil Rights Champions
Charismatic Cult Leaders
Courageous Crimefighters
Environmental Pioneers
Great Auto Makers and Their Cars
Great Justices of the Supreme Court
Hatemongers and Demagogues
Hoaxers and Hustlers
International Terrorists
Journalists Who Made History
Legendary Labor Leaders
Philanthropists and Their Legacies
Soviet Leaders from Lenin to Gorbachev
Top Entrepreneurs and Their Businesses
Top Lawyers and Their Famous Cases
Treacherous Traitors
Utopian Visionaries
Women Business Leaders
Women Chosen for Public Office
Women in Medicine
Women Inventors and Their Discoveries
Women of the U.S. Congress
Women Who Led Nations
Women Who Reformed Politics
The World's Greatest Explorers

WOMEN WHO LED NATIONS

Joan Axelrod-Contrada

The Oliver Press, Inc.
Minneapolis

The Oliver Press, Inc.
Charlotte Square
5707 West 36th Street
Minneapolis, MN 55416-2510

Library of Congress Cataloging-in-Publication Data

Axelrod-Contrada, Joan
Women who led nations / Joan Axelrod-Contrada
p.   cm.—(Profiles ; ISSN 28)
Includes bibliographical references and index.
      Summary: Profiles the careers of seven women elected to head
their respective countries, including Golda Meir, Indira Gandhi,
Margaret Thatcher, Corazón Aquino, Benazir Bhutto, Violeta Barrios
de Chamorro, and Gro Harlem Brundtland.
ISBN 1-881508-48-X (library binding)
1. Women heads of state—Biography—Juvenile literature.
2. Women in politics—Juvenile literature. 3. Women—Biography—
Juvenile literature. [1. Women presidents. 2. Women prime
ministers. 3. Presidents. 4. Prime ministers. 5. Women in politics.
6. Women—Biography.] I. Title. II. Series: Profiles (Minneapolis,
Minn.) ; 28.
D839.5.A94   1999
920.72—dc21
[B]   98-10958
                                                         CIP
                                                          AC

ISBN 1-881508-48-X
Printed in the United States of America
05 04 03 02 01 00 99   8 7 6 5 4 3 2 1

Contents

Elected after her husband, the prime minister of Sri Lanka, was slain, Sirimavo Bandaranaike led her country for two terms, 1960-1965 and 1970-1977.

Introduction

*W*hile queens and empresses ruled even in ancient times, only in the last half of the twentieth century have women been democratically elected to lead nations. Prime Minister Sirimavo Bandaranaike of Sri Lanka made history in 1960 when she became the first woman elected to lead a nation.

In many countries, laws prevented women from holding office or voting. Not until the nineteenth century did the idea of women's rights grow into an organized movement, now known as *feminism*, for the political, economic, and social equality of women with men.

In 1893, New Zealand became the first country to grant the right to vote to both men and women. In the twentieth century, women around the globe began to gain the right to vote. Among the earliest countries to give

During a 1912 New York City parade, American women marched to persuade the government to grant them the right to vote.

women voting rights were Australia (1901), Finland (1906), Norway (1913), Britain (1918-1928), and the United States (1920). In some newly formed nations, women could vote alongside men from the start: 1947 in Pakistan and 1948 in Israel. In the Philippines, women won the right to vote in 1939, Indian women gained the vote in 1950, and Nicaraguan women became voters in 1955. By the year 1998, women had gained the vote everywhere except in six Middle Eastern countries and in the tiny nation of Brunei Darussalam in Southeast Asia.

Winning the legal right to cast votes, however, has proved a much easier task for women than capturing votes as candidates. In 1998, the United Nations reported that women held only 7 percent of the high-level elected and appointed offices in governments around the world.

While women in some cultures—the North American Algonquin Indians, for instance—have always played prominent roles in public life, those in many other societies have traditionally been expected to remain at home while their husbands and sons achieved success in the outside world. Not surprisingly, some women leaders have risen to power by extending these supportive family roles. Although this book profiles only democratically elected heads of state, four of these women won election because they came from prominent political families. Prime Minister Indira Gandhi of India, President Corazón Aquino of the Philippines, President Violeta Barrios de Chamorro of Nicaragua, and Prime Minister Benazir Bhutto of Pakistan all followed the footsteps of their famous fathers or husbands into office.

Indira Gandhi was the daughter of India's first prime minister, Jawaharlal Nehru. Although party bosses called her a "dumb doll" behind her back, they chose her as their leader in 1966 because of her famous name and familiar face. Little did they know she would turn out to be a powerful and, at times, autocratic ruler.

Corazón Aquino, too, surprised those who thought the Philippines needed a man as its leader. The widow of slain opposition leader Benigno Aquino Jr., she presided over the "people power" revolution that toppled the regime of Philippine dictator Ferdinand Marcos in February 1986, restoring democracy to the Philippines.

In 1988, Benazir Bhutto, the daughter of executed Pakistani head of state Zulfikar Ali Bhutto, rose to power as the first Muslim woman in the world to become prime minister. In a country in which women traditionally stay at home and wear heavy veils in public, the Western-educated Bhutto waged a winning campaign to carry on her father's legacy.

Nicaraguan Violeta Barrios de Chamorro, the widow of slain newspaper publisher Pedro Joaquin Chamorro, ended the civil war in her country after she was elected president in 1990. In a culture long known for its *machismo*, or the idea that men must be extremely aggressive, virile, and brave, Violeta preached the politics of reconciliation.

As the heirs of political family dynasties, Gandhi, Aquino, Bhutto, and Chamorro enjoyed the advantage of having built-in power bases and fundraising. Nevertheless, in the past 40 years, candidates from humbler circumstances have also become leaders. Golda Meir of Israel, Margaret Thatcher of Great Britain, and Gro Harlem Brundtland of Norway came to power not as political heirs but as proven leaders in their own right.

Golda Meir used her abilities as an organizer and an orator to help build the new nation of Israel, which was created in 1948. Later, in 1969, she became prime minister and led Israel through some difficult years.

In 1979, Margaret Thatcher, too, held her own in the mostly male Parliament to become prime minister of Britain. Nicknamed the "Iron Lady" for her strong stand against Communism, she set her nation on a conservative

British prime minister Margaret Thatcher and U.S. president Ronald Reagan set similar economic goals for their countries during the 1980s: reduction of government spending and regulations, lower taxes, and encouragement of free enterprise.

The United States has yet to choose a woman as president. In 1984, Democratic congresswoman Geraldine Ferraro became the first woman ever selected by a major political party as a vice-presidential candidate. She and her running mate, presidential candidate Walter Mondale, lost the election, but women have continued to run for other offices. In 1998, they occupied 55 seats in the U.S. House of Representatives and 9 in the Senate, 11 percent of the total number of legislators. Women made up an even larger proportion of state legislatures, averaging 21 percent.

path emphasizing personal responsibility and free-market economic competition.

In 1986, newly elected Prime Minister Gro Harlem Brundtland of Norway appointed 8 women to her 18-member cabinet—the highest percentage of women in key government posts in the world. A well-known feminist and environmentalist, Brundtland maintained that men need to shoulder more home and childcare responsibilities so that women can achieve equal opportunity in the workplace.

The seven women profiled in this book varied greatly in their political philosophies and personal styles. Some belonged to liberal groups trying to eliminate social injustices, while others identified more with conservative parties upholding the values of the past. Some aligned themselves with feminism, while others would not have called themselves feminists.

Despite their different backgrounds, each of these leaders overcame significant bias against her gender and rose to the top of her nation. And each served as a powerful role model for women around the world. Although each woman faced challenges unique to her own nation, all demonstrated great courage and determination.

A stirring orator and tireless organizer, Golda Meir (1898-1978) used her talents and energy to help create a new country for the Jewish people—and then became its leader in 1969.

1

Golda Meir
Israeli Pioneer and Prime Minister

*L*ate one night in May 1948, a Jewish woman embarked on a secret mission. Disguised as an Arab in black robes and a veil, Golda Meir crossed the border into Jordan to persuade King Abdullah to accept a new nation for the Jewish people.

King Abdullah, pressured by other Arab leaders to join them in opposing a Jewish state, wanted the Jews to delay their plans.

"Why are you in such a hurry to proclaim your state?" he asked Meir through a translator.

"In a hurry?" she replied. "A people that has waited 2,000 years can hardly be described as being in a hurry."

Although the mission failed and Jordan soon joined in an Arab war against the new nation of Israel, Meir, who would serve as prime minister from 1969 until 1974, never lost sight of her hopes for peace in the Middle East. She insisted, however, that the Jews not sacrifice their homeland. The Jews had worked too hard—and suffered too long—to lose that.

Meir knew about suffering. The second surviving child of Bluma and Moshe Mabovitch, she was born on May 3, 1898, in Kiev, Russia. Her sister, Sheyna, was nine years older. Five other Mabovitch children had died while still infants. Golda was named for her great-grandmother Golde, a strong-willed woman who took her tea with salt instead of sugar to remind herself of the bitter taste of living without a Jewish homeland.

Jews in Russia in the late 1800s and early 1900s needed to be strong to cope with the discrimination they faced. Soldiers of the Tsar, the ruler of Russia, sometimes rode their horses through the poor Jewish villages, setting off rampages of murder and destruction called *pogroms*.

When Golda was four, her father boarded up the windows of the family's one-room apartment in anticipation of violence. That pogrom never occurred, but, although only a child, Golda knew the barricades would not have protected them.

In 1903, Moshe Mabovitch sold all his belongings, even the tools that he used to earn his living, and sailed for America. Bluma and the three girls (Zipke was born in 1901) stayed behind in Russia. Three years later, Moshe sent for them to join him in Milwaukee, Wisconsin, where he had found work with a railroad company. In Milwaukee, Bluma opened a small grocery store. Despite the long hours she worked helping her mother in the store, Golda was a straight-A student.

At the age of 11, Golda organized her first political meeting. The public school she attended was free, but students had to buy their own books. Some families could not afford to purchase the texts for their children, a situation Golda thought was unjust. Although Bluma urged her to write out her speech for the meeting, Golda instead spoke from her heart, a technique she would use throughout her career. She spoke in plain but emotional terms. This first appeal, like many that would follow in her adult years, was successful, and she raised enough money to purchase the needed books.

As Golda reached adolescence, she, like her older sister, Sheyna, rebelled against her strict parents. Golda wanted to go to high school, but Bluma and Moshe believed that too much education could ruin a girl's prospects for marriage.

Golda wrote a long letter to Sheyna, who was living in Denver, Colorado, with her husband, Sam Korngold. The couple urged Golda to come and stay with them.

Golda saved the money she earned from wrapping packages in a department store and teaching English to recent immigrants. One morning, instead of going to school, she left a note for her parents and picked up a suitcase she had hidden at a friend's house. Fourteen-year-old Golda then bought a train ticket to Denver.

The Korngolds' apartment was a gathering place for young intellectuals from Russia who spoke about combining the economic equality of Socialism with the Jewish nationalism of Zionism. Since the late 1800s, Zionists had been working to build a homeland for Jews in what was then called Palestine but would later become Israel. One evening, a quiet, bespectacled sign painter named Morris Meyerson joined Sheyna's discussion group. Morris was less interested in politics than in art, music, and literature. Before long, he and Golda fell in love.

About eighteen months later, Golda's father wrote, urging her to come home because Bluma missed her greatly. Golda returned to Milwaukee in 1914 with the understanding that she be allowed to complete high school and train to become a teacher. Morris remained in Denver but promised to write to Golda every day.

World War I, meanwhile, was sweeping across Europe, and the Mabovitch household in Milwaukee was alive with war news and political discussions. Increasingly, Golda's life revolved around Zionism. She gave speeches about Jewish causes on street corners and in front of synagogues. Although Moshe, too, was a Zionist, he considered it improper for a girl to be speaking on the street. One day, he followed Golda, threatening to bring her home "by her hair." Instead, he stayed and listened to her speak, amazed by her ability.

With the aid of the Arabs, the British gained control of Palestine during World War I. Together, they defeated the Ottoman Empire, which had ruled Palestine since

Golda Mabovitch, second from right in the back row, pictured with a group of fellow schoolteachers. She graduated from a teachers college in 1916 when she was 18 years old.

1516. The empire had also controlled sections of the Middle East, Eastern Europe, and North Africa. Today, the modern nation of Turkey is all that remains of the mighty Ottoman Empire.

British foreign secretary Lord Arthur Balfour announced that Britain favored the creation of a national homeland for the Jews in Palestine. Britain also promised to support the civil and religious rights of non-Jewish Palestinians. (The League of Nations, a forerunner of the United Nations, later formally granted Great Britain the right to govern Palestine.) Golda's dream of a Jewish homeland was one step closer to reality.

Morris, however, lacked Golda's enthusiasm for Zionism. After Golda let him know in no uncertain terms that, with or without him, she planned to settle in Palestine, he finally agreed to go. On December 24, 1917, Golda and Morris were married, and they pledged to move to Palestine in their wedding vows. Following their marriage, Golda quit teaching and began to work for the Labor Zionist Party, traveling across the United States to raise money and organize new groups. After saving for four years, the Meyersons purchased tickets to Palestine.

On May 23, 1921, Golda and Morris set sail along with Sheyna and her two children. They would later be joined by Sheyna's husband, Sam, and their younger sister, Zipke. After a harrowing sea journey during which the mutinous crew sabotaged the engines, set fires, and salted the passengers' drinking water, they arrived in Italy.

Then, their luggage disappeared while they were waiting to board a ship to Egypt. From Alexandria, the pioneers took a train to Palestine, arriving in Tel Aviv on July 14, 1921.

"Only here could Jews be masters, not victims of their fate," Golda wrote. "So it was not surprising . . . I was profoundly happy."

Golda wanted to live on Kibbutz Merhavia, but kibbutz members rejected her at first because they assumed she was a "spoiled American," unable to perform the hard physical labor. After meeting Golda and Morris, however, the kibbutz members changed their minds.

In the egalitarian environment of Merhavia, women were freed from their traditional homemaker roles. They shared in the governing of the kibbutz and worked alongside men in the fields. Unlike many women in the kibbutz movement, however, Golda enjoyed the kitchen work, asking "Why is it so much better to work in the barn and feed cows, rather than in the kitchen and feed your comrades?"

Golda thrived on the hard labor and camaraderie of kibbutz life, entering the political arena as Merhavia's representative to the Histadrut, a labor federation for Jewish workers in Palestine. Morris, however, languished, unhappy and in poor health. He insisted that if Golda wanted children, they must raise them themselves rather than stay on the kibbutz where they would be raised cooperatively. Sadly, after two years, Golda left Merhavia.

The couple moved briefly to Tel Aviv, then to a small apartment in Jerusalem. In 1924, Golda gave birth to a son, Menachem, and to a daughter, Sarah, in 1926. Morris worked as a bookkeeper, and Golda took in laundry from Menachem's nursery school to pay for his tuition. But Golda disliked being confined to the private world of the home. Feeling sidelined from the struggle to create a new society, she knew she was not cut out to be a traditional wife and mother.

Finally, in 1928, Golda Meyerson applied for a position as secretary of the women's labor council of the Histadrut. Over the years, the Histadrut had transformed itself from a labor union into the unofficial government of the Jews in Palestine. Her new position required her to move to Tel Aviv. Golda and Morris separated, but they remained friends until Morris's death in 1951.

Golda Meyerson, who later changed her name to Meir, traveled extensively for the Histadrut. Usually, she left Menachem and Sarah with Sheyna or her parents, who had emigrated in 1926. She rose from the women's council to the inner circle of the Histadrut and became head of its political department in 1936.

Meir's talents for speaking and administration, as well as her ability to work long, hard hours, earned her the respect of the men in the organization. Yet she often felt guilty about being away from her children. "I think . . . that women who want and need a life outside as well as inside the home have a much, much harder time than men because they carry such a heavy double burden," she later wrote.

While the Jewish pioneers in Palestine were creating new homes, the Jews in Nazi Germany during the 1930s were persecuted and many were sent to concentration camps. Many Jews fled Europe, about 60,000 of them to Palestine. Some Arabs there, feeling threatened and angered by this influx of Jews, overturned buses and trains and set fire to Jewish fields and homes.

The British, however, still ruled Palestine. In an attempt to soothe Arab concerns about being overpowered by the Jews, the British, in the late summer of 1939, issued a government policy that sharply limited the immigration of European Jews into Palestine. More than 20 other countries also closed their doors to Jews fleeing Nazi persecution. When World War II began in September, millions of Jews were trapped in Europe. Before Germany and its allied countries were defeated in 1945, six million Jews died in concentration camps in what became known as the Holocaust.

Mourning the devastating losses of the Holocaust, the Jewish community in Palestine, many of whose members had fought for the British during the war, now resolved to free themselves from British rule. They smuggled in as many refugees as they could. In 1946, the British arrested David Ben-Gurion and other prominent Zionist leaders. With Ben-Gurion in prison, Golda Meir assumed leadership of the Jewish community.

Millions of Jewish people suffered in concentration camps during the murderous years of the Nazi regime, which lasted from 1933 to 1945.

By February 1947, Britain despaired of trying to govern Palestine and turned the problem over to the United Nations. On November 29, 1947, the United Nations voted to partition Palestine into two states—one Jewish, the other Arab. Ben-Gurion and the other prisoners were released. The Arabs, meanwhile, were so angered by the impending formation of the new Jewish nation of Israel that they threatened war.

On May 14, 1948, Golda Meir and 24 other leaders signed a declaration of independence for the new nation of Israel. War followed immediately, as King Abdullah had predicted. Meir set out on a whirlwind tour of the U.S. to raise money for arms and returned with an extraordinary $50 million. The part of Palestine promised for an Arab nation was swallowed up by Israel, Egypt, and Jordan. Palestinians fled to refugee camps.

Zionist leader David Ben-Gurion surrounded by the soldiers who went to war with their Arab neighbors shortly after Ben-Gurion's announcement of Israel's nationhood in May 1948

The government the Israelis set up consisted of a legislature, called the Knesset, composed of 120 members elected every four years by all citizens. The Knesset elects a president, who then selects a prime minister to lead the country from among Knesset members, usually the head of the political party with the most representatives. The prime minister chooses a cabinet of advisers.

Meir served as ambassador to Russia during 1948 and 1949 under David Ben-Gurion, who had become Israel's first prime minister. Then she returned to Israel to take a seat in the Knesset and served as minister of labor from 1949 to 1956. As Jews flocked to their new homeland from all over the world, Meir oversaw the development of 30,000 new housing units as well as job training for new citizens. She later said that the seven years she worked as minister of labor were "without doubt, the most satisfying and happiest in my life."

In 1956, Golda Meir was appointed foreign minister. Ben-Gurion asked all his cabinet members to use Hebrew names. This was when she chose to be called Meir, meaning "to illuminate." In her new position, Meir helped negotiate an end to Israel's 1956 conflict with Egypt over the Suez Canal and also initiated a policy of technical assistance to developing nations in Africa and Asia.

Meir resigned her position in the cabinet in 1965. She enjoyed her retirement, reading, cooking Jewish specialties such as chicken soup and gefilte fish, and taking care of her five grandchildren.

Golda Meir served as Israel's foreign minister for nine years, 1956-1965. During that time, she often presented her country's position at the United Nations, as shown here.

In 1966 and 1967, tensions flared between Israel and its Arab neighbors—Egypt, Syria, and Jordan. War broke out on June 5, 1967. Israel quickly overran the Arab forces in what became known as the Six-Day War, enlarging its borders to include the Sinai Peninsula, the Gaza Strip, and the Golan Heights of Syria, as well as capturing the Arab section of Jerusalem.

In February 1969, Israel's prime minister Levi Eshkol died suddenly of a heart attack. The Labor Party chose 70-year-old Meir to serve as prime minister until a new election could be held. That election, held in October 1969, saw Meir lead her party to victory. Newspaper reporters called her "Israel's Uncrowned Queen."

As prime minister, Meir advocated a strong defense. She persuaded U.S. president Richard Nixon to send arms to protect Israel against an Arab attack. During her tenure, Arab terrorists set off bombs, hijacked airplanes, and also murdered Israeli athletes at the 1972 Olympic games in Munich, Germany.

While prime minister, Golda Meir found in U.S. president Richard Nixon a strong supporter of Israel.

Meir wanted peace but insisted that Israel not return to its pre-1967 boundaries. Maintaining that Arabs who wanted to eliminate Israel left no room for compromise, she dismissed the demands of Palestinian refugees for a homeland. The Arabs did not need another nation, she said. Critics of her strong stance called her "intransigent," which means refusing to compromise. She joked that intransigent had become her middle name.

Meanwhile, Meir secretly negotiated with King Hussein of Jordan with hopes of peace, but to no avail. She also met with Pope Paul VI in 1973. The pope asked Meir how a people as merciful as the Jews could behave so fiercely in their own country. "When we were merciful," she replied, "we were led to the gas chambers."

Golda Meir was famous around the world for her homespun style. On Saturday nights, she met at home with her top advisers, dubbed her Kitchen Cabinet. Sometimes she would interrupt meetings to ask visitors if they would prefer one lump of sugar or two in their tea.

In autumn 1973, Meir asked her advisers to look into rumors of a pending Arab attack on Israel. Upon being told there was nothing to worry about, she decided not to mobilize the Israeli army.

Violence erupted on Yom Kippur, the holiest day of the Jewish year. When many citizens were praying and fasting on October 6, the Arabs launched a surprise attack. More than 2,000 Israeli soldiers died in the fighting, and an estimated 8,000 were wounded. Many blamed

Two Jerusalem landmarks: The Dome of the Rock and the Wailing Wall

LEBANON

Golan Heights

SYRIA

Mediterranean Sea

•Tel-Aviv

West Bank

Jerusalem⊙

Dead Sea

Gaza Strip

ISRAEL

JORDAN

EGYPT

SAUDI ARABIA

ISRAEL

Capital: Jerusalem
Area: 8, 015 square miles
Population: 5,535,000
Languages: Hebrew, Arabic, Yiddish, English
Religion: 82% Jewish, 13% Muslim, 2% Christian

Voting Age: All citizens age 18 and over
Currency: Shekel
Gross Domestic Product Per Person: $15,500
Literacy rate: 92%
Life Expectancy: 78 female, 74 male

Meir for the heavy casualties and for agreeing to what some saw as a premature cease-fire with the Arabs on October 24. Racked with guilt, she took responsibility for the war. Although reelected prime minister in December 1973, Meir resigned in April 1974.

Golda Meir spent the next few years lecturing and writing her autobiography. She visited the United States, returning to her former elementary school in Milwaukee where she had raised money to buy books so many years before. She said the students treated her "like a queen," singing songs for her in Yiddish and Hebrew.

Meir's health, though, was failing. She had kept her cancer secret during her years as prime minister, but now it had spread. Golda Meir died at the age of 80 on December 8, 1978, with her children and younger sister at her bedside.

Shortly before her death, Israeli prime minister Menachem Begin and Egyptian president Anwar Sadat were announced as the Nobel Peace Prize winners for 1978. Meir lamented in private that her own peace efforts had gone largely unrecognized. In a letter of sympathy to her children after her death, however, Sadat credited Meir with starting the peace process.

In her autobiography, Golda Meir recounted a recurrent dream she had in which Arabs crossed the border into Israel driving tractors instead of tanks. People throughout the world hope that her dream of peace will one day become a reality.

*The public personality of Indian prime minister
Indira Gandhi (1917-1984) was as large and
complex as the country she governed.*

2

Indira Gandhi
Mother to India

*I*ndira Nehru Gandhi considered it her destiny to lead India. Although no relation to the legendary Mohandas "Mahatma" Gandhi, who led the movement for India's independence from Great Britain, Indira grew up with politics in her blood. Her father, Jawaharlal Nehru, was the Mahatma's right-hand man in the independence movement and served as India's first prime minister from 1947 until 1964.

Indira Gandhi acquired her last name—a fairly common one in India—through her marriage to journalist

Feroze Gandhi, and she rose to power on her father's coattails. Once in office, however, she proved a formidable leader in her own right.

Indira Gandhi was a woman of many contradictions: sometimes warm and self-effacing, sometimes chilly and aloof—a lonely woman adored by the masses. Although schooled in the Mahatma's philosophy of nonviolence, she sometimes resorted to force. For nearly two decades, she unified a poor, chaotic, and religiously divided nation that included 746 million people by 1984—the most populous democracy in the world.

Roughly 83 percent of Indians follow Hinduism, a religion probably best known for grouping people into social classes called *castes*. A Hindu is born into a caste that determines his or her social status and often occupation as well. Other religions in India include Islam, Christianity, and Sikhism, which blends the teachings of Hinduism and Islam. Although Buddhism began in India about 500 years before Christ and spread throughout Asia, today only about 1 percent of Indians are Buddhists.

At the time of Indira Gandhi's birth in 1917, the British ruled India. Britain's involvement in the country dated back to the seventeenth century when a prominent British firm, the East India Company, established several fortified trading posts in India. In 1858, the British government took over India from the East India Company.

Under British rule, native Indians had fewer rights and privileges than their rulers. Considering this unfair, many Indians demanded a greater role in government. Under the leadership of Mohandas Gandhi and Jawaharlal Nehru, an advisory body known as the Indian National Congress became the voice of an independence movement seeking to free India from British colonial rule.

Born on November 19, 1917, in Allahabad, a large city in central India, Indira Priyadarshini Nehru was the only child of Kamala and Jawaharlal Nehru. As members of the elite Brahman caste of Hindus, the Nehrus were a wealthy and influential family. Indira grew up on a palatial estate built by her grandfather Motilal Nehru, which was called the "House of Joy." But, because Indira was often left behind with the servants while her parents, grandfather, aunts, and cousins spent time in prison for their opposition to British rule, Indira's childhood was more lonely than joyful. She cherished the long letters her father wrote to her from prison.

When Indira was three years old, the Nehrus built a fire in their courtyard and destroyed their foreign-made belongings in a blaze of nationalistic pride. The family refused to buy or wear imported goods and they abandoned their extravagant way of life to embrace the spartan simplicity of the independence movement. Young Indira even burned her favorite foreign-made doll. "I felt as if I was murdering someone," she later recalled.

At the age of 12, Indira formed her own children's political group, the Monkey Brigade. The children ran errands, spied on the British police, and performed other tasks to help their parents in the Indian National Congress.

In 1934, Indira attended a special university called Santiniketan, where she studied Indian arts and nature. But, after only a year and a half, she left for Switzerland

Indira (standing) photographed with her parents Jawaharlal (left) and Kamala Nehru in 1931. By this time, the entire Nehru family was involved in India's independence movement.

with her mother, who was sick with tuberculosis. Despite the medical care she received there, Kamala died in 1936.

Indira credited her mother with teaching her to speak Hindi like a native (Jawaharlal, in contrast, spoke Hindi with an English accent) and passing on her "Indianness," even though she was ridiculed by the more sophisticated, Westernized women in the Nehru extended family. "I saw her being hurt and I was determined not to be hurt," Indira remembered.

After her mother's death, Indira went to England where she studied modern history at Somerville College in Oxford. In 1941, she returned to India, accompanied by a family friend named Feroze Gandhi, who had been courting her in England. They married on March 26, 1942.

That September, Indira Gandhi was arrested while speaking at a public meeting. After celebrating her 25th birthday in prison with an aunt and cousin, who were also political prisoners, she was released in May 1943. In August 1944, she gave birth to her first child, Rajiv. A second son, Sanjay, followed in December 1946.

The struggle for independence, meanwhile, had heated up. In early 1946, Great Britain had offered to grant India its independence as soon as the people agreed on a form of government. Although the largely Hindu Indian National Congress was still at the forefront of the independence movement, followers of Islam, known as Muslims, began pushing for a nation of their own to be called Pakistan, which means "Land of the Pure."

Despite Mohandas Gandhi's pleas for unity, the region was partitioned into two separate countries. The northeast and northwest sections, populated predominantly by Muslims, became West and East Pakistan—a single nation that was separated by more than 1,000 miles. (East Pakistan would later split and become the independent country of Bangladesh.) The much larger India, mostly Hindu, sprawled between the two sections of Pakistan. The Indian National Congress became the Congress Party, India's foremost political machine.

On August 15, 1947, India became an independent country with a parliamentary system of government. Parliament meets at the capital, New Delhi, in northern India. It consists of two houses, Lok Sabha—the House of the People, elected directly by the voters—and Rajya Sabha—the Council of States, elected by the 25 state legislatures. The leader of the political party with the most seats in Parliament becomes prime minister and chooses a cabinet. A president serves as the country's head of state, but the prime minister actually leads the government.

Jawaharlal Nehru became India's first prime minister. Seeing that her father needed help, Indira Gandhi moved back into his house in New Delhi with her two sons to serve as his official host as well as unofficial adviser. Feroze, the managing director of a newspaper, stayed in Lucknow. Their marriage suffered as a result.

"When I went into public life and became successful, he [Feroze] liked it and he didn't like it," Indira

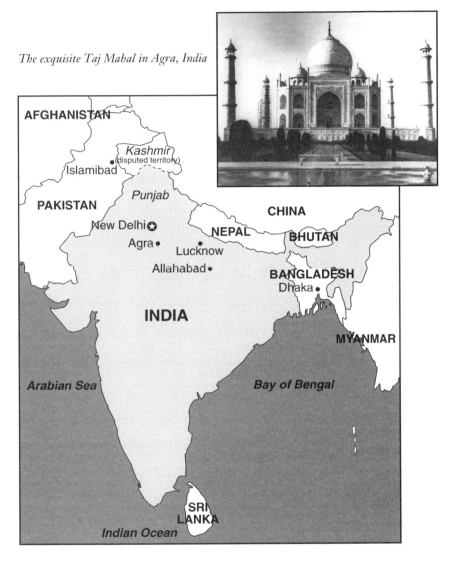

The exquisite Taj Mahal in Agra, India

AFGHANISTAN

Kashmir
(disputed territory)

Islamibad

PAKISTAN

Punjab

CHINA

New Delhi

NEPAL

BHUTAN

Agra

Lucknow

Allahabad

BANGLADESH

Dhaka

INDIA

MYANMAR

Arabian Sea

Bay of Bengal

SRI
LANKA

Indian Ocean

INDIA

Capital: New Delhi
Area: 1,237,062 square miles
Population: 966,780,000
Languages: English, Hindi, Telugu, Bengali
Religion: 80% Hindu, 14% Muslim, 2% Christian, 2% Sikh

Voting Age: All citizens age 18 and over
Currency: Rupee
Gross Domestic Product Per Person: $1,500
Literacy rate: 52%
Life Expectancy: 61 female, 60 male

Gandhi recalled. "Other people—friends, relatives—were the worst. They would say, 'How does it feel, being so-and-so's husband?' He would get upset, and it would take me weeks to win him over." Feroze Gandhi later entered politics as well, serving as a member of parliament from 1952 until his death in 1960.

As "the nation's daughter," Indira Gandhi accompanied her father everywhere, helping him give parties and dinners. She disliked the crowds and the lack of privacy, but she endured them because India always came first, ahead of her own needs. Although she knew everyone in political circles, she had no official government position and no one took her seriously.

Then, in 1955, Gandhi acquired some power of her own as a member of a Congress Party working committee. Four years later, she became president of the Congress Party. Displaying a toughness surprising for someone so long overshadowed by her father, Gandhi weeded out ineffectual party members, negotiated agreements among rival factions, and helped defeat a Communist state government. But, after just a year, she left her post to devote all her energies to caring for her ailing father, who was now in his seventies.

One night in January 1964, Nehru suffered a stroke and collapsed in his daughter's arms. For the next four months, Gandhi nursed him and helped him run the country from his sickbed. Nehru believed too strongly in his democratic ideals to request that his daughter be

Indira Gandhi was at her father's side during many state occasions, including this visit to Moscow in June 1955. Nikita Khrushchev, then secretary general of the Communist Party of the Soviet Union, stands to the right of Indira; Soviet premier Nikolai Bulganin (wearing a hat) is on the right.

named his successor. When he died that May, Lal Bahadur Shastri became India's second prime minister. Shastri appointed Gandhi minister of information and broadcasting. Less than two years later, Shastri died suddenly of a heart attack, leaving Congress Party leaders unable to agree on a successor.

Thinking that Nehru's obedient daughter would be easy to control, party bosses chose her as their leader. Behind her back, they called her a "dumb doll." On January 19, 1966, at the age of 48, Indira Gandhi became India's first female prime minister. Few people predicted that she would develop into a shrewd politician.

At first, Gandhi seemed unclear about what to do. But when the economy sank into a recession, and agricultural shortages threatened millions of Indians with starvation, she imported grain from America.

As a woman in politics, the prime minister felt that she had to work twice as hard as a man in the same position. And, as Nehru's daughter, she worked even harder to be seen as a leader in her own right. Still, Gandhi also won the adoration of many simply by virtue of being Nehru's daughter.

The prime minister projected a charisma in public that seemed out of keeping with her shyness. In a nation as vast and diverse as India, the top leader had enormous symbolic importance. Gandhi traveled the country widely to see the people. She clearly empathized with the masses, particularly the poor and the powerless. When she visited a group of women victimized by higher caste men, she sat on the ground and listened to their stories. Women had equal rights under the law, but centuries of religious tradition kept them subordinate to men.

After winning the 1967 elections, Indira Gandhi nationalized the commercial banks and launched a Green

Revolution to make India agriculturally self-sufficient through the increased use of fertilizers, irrigation, and other more efficient farming practices. She reasserted—sometimes forcefully—the dominance of the central government over the states. She also defended herself against a call for her resignation by members of the conservative opposition within her own party.

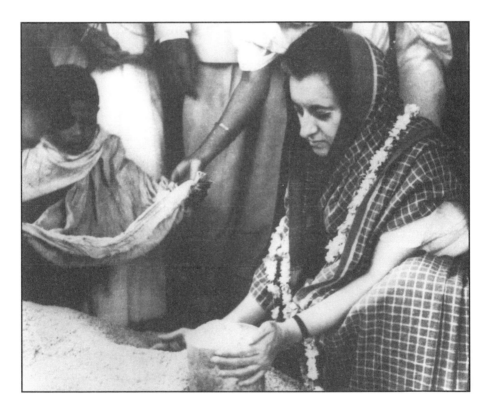

Prime Minister Indira Gandhi distributed rice during a drought. Feeding all the citizens of India, the most populous democracy in the world, was one of many challenges Gandhi faced.

The Congress Party had divided into two factions. The older members rallied around conservative Morarji Desai, while the younger, more radical members supported Gandhi. She won a resounding victory in the March 1971 elections.

Indira Gandhi had little time to celebrate. India became involved in a civil war between the two sections of Pakistan. Later that year, on December 3, 1971, West Pakistan bombed eight Indian airfields, hoping to prevent Indian interference in the Pakistani dispute. The tactic backfired, and Gandhi dispatched troops to East Pakistan to help it win independence from the western section of the country. Within two weeks, the Indian troops triumphed. East Pakistan became the independent nation of Bangladesh, and India was now recognized as the predominant power in the region.

During Gandhi's tenure, India tested its first atomic bomb. The country also launched a satellite into space and built up its armed forces with Soviet weaponry. In 1973, the London *Sunday Times* hailed Indira Gandhi as "The Most Powerful Woman in the World." That same year, she launched Project Tiger, an effort to save the animal and preserve its habitat. "The tiger's future is our future," she said. Her program also provided new sources of water, which benefited people as well as tigers.

But India's problems remained daunting. After declaring "Abolish Poverty" as her campaign pledge in 1971, the prime minister had failed to make good on her promise, causing her political opponents to accuse her of empty sloganeering. The costs of the Pakistani war sent the economy into another downward spin. Riots erupted. The ruling Congress Party was badly divided, and many considered it corrupt. Gandhi cut herself off from good advice and installed puppet leaders in many of the regions. India's population, meanwhile, continued to swell.

Then in 1975, a court in Allahabad convicted Gandhi of breaking election laws during her 1971 campaign and canceled her election to Parliament. She was guilty of using government vehicles and employees during the campaign. The conviction was a sharp political blow. Opponents now clamored for her resignation.

Seeing herself as indispensible to India's welfare, the prime minister refused to step down. Instead, on June 26, 1975, Gandhi sent dozens of opposition leaders to prison. About 100,000 other opponents and protesters soon followed them to jail. Declaring a state of emergency, she suspended civil liberties, such as the right to protest or strike as well as freedom of the press. Wages were frozen. Critics accused the prime minister of turning her back on democracy and becoming a dictator. Gandhi, however, insisted that she was simply protecting the rights of the majority. "In India, democracy has given too much license to people," she claimed. "Sometimes a bitter medicine has to be administered to a patient to cure him."

Gandhi's son Sanjay became her chief adviser. Surrounding himself with a group of young toughs,

Sanjay initiated a population-control program that promoted sterilization. Rumors of forced sterilizations provoked often violent public protests against the program. To clean up the cities, he moved people living in the worst slums and destroyed their homes without providing other places for them to go.

Gandhi scheduled new elections for March 1977, hoping a victory would vindicate her actions. As her campaign theme, she proclaimed, "Only a strong central government can build a stronger India." The Janata Party, a coalition of several opposition parties, countered with a banner that read, "End Dictatorship. Dethrone the Queen."

On March 20, 1977, the people of India voted Gandhi out of office. Her old nemesis, conservative Morarji Desai, emerged from prison to become prime minister. Indira Gandhi was arrested on a charge of corruption and released; then she was arrested and released again.

Throughout the turmoil, she continued to enjoy widespread popular support, showing that, for all her faults, she was still a widely revered public figure. Thousands of Indians protested Gandhi's arrests. The political coalition against her crumbled as members fought among themselves and failed to address any of India's pressing problems. Gandhi formed her own break-away party, the Congress (I) Party, and campaigned vigorously for reelection.

Indira Gandhi's longtime political opponent Morarji Desai led India from 1977-79.

When the nation voted in January 1980, Gandhi once again scored an impressive victory. Having given up her office freely after the previous election, she returned with her reputation largely intact. Now a national heroine, known to millions as "Mother" or "Madam" or even just "She," crowds everywhere shouted "Long live Indira!"

Then, on June 23, 1980, Sanjay died in a plane crash. An avid pilot, he had been flying too low while performing a stunt. The grief-stricken prime minister began grooming her elder son, Rajiv, to succeed her.

In 1983, violence flared between Hindus and Muslims in response to a government decision allowing Muslim immigrants from Pakistan to vote in state elections. At least 2,000 people, mostly Muslims, were killed in the worst fighting between the two groups since 1947. Gandhi spoke out against the centuries-old religious rivalries dividing the nation.

Compounding the tensions were demands for more power by the followers of Sikhism, a religion that combined aspects of Hinduism and Islam. In the northwest state of Punjab, Sikh terrorists turned the Golden Temple, their most sacred shrine, into a fortress in the hopes of starting their own nation. Gandhi dispatched troops to squelch the rebellion. On June 6, 1984, Indian soldiers stormed the stronghold, killing nearly 1,000 people and damaging the temple.

On the morning of October 31, 1984, two of Gandhi's own bodyguards, both Sikhs whom she trusted, shot her in revenge for ordering the attack on the Golden Temple. The 66-year-old prime minister died later that day. In her will, Gandhi had made clear her love for India, writing, "No hate is dark enough to overshadow the extent of my love for my people and my country."

Indira Gandhi remains, by far, the best-known woman in Indian politics. Although she undoubtedly had her weaknesses, she increased agricultural production, enhanced India's role as a world power, and developed a remarkable relationship with her people. For millions of Indians, India was Indira, and Indira was India.

Following Gandhi's death, her son, Rajiv, was elected party leader and became prime minister. He headed India until the Congress Party was swept from power in the

Rajiv Gandhi (1944-1991) was a pilot for Indian Airlines until elected to fill his brother's seat in Parliament, left vacant by Sanjay's death in 1980. During his four years as prime minister, Rajiv attempted to curb corruption and revive the Congress Party.

November 1989 elections. Rajiv Gandhi was killed in May 1991 while campaigning for reelection, the victim of a terrorist bomb. His assassin, a young woman who had concealed the bomb in her clothing, as well as at least 15 bystanders also died in the blast.

The name Gandhi still holds tremendous sway in India. As the nation continues to struggle with social and political unrest, many Indians are looking to Rajiv's widow, Sonia Gandhi, for leadership. She was elected president of India's Congress Party in March 1998, but the opposing Janata Party won more seats in the election and formed the next government.

Margaret Thatcher (b.1925) was Britain's first woman prime minister as well as that country's longest-serving prime minister in the twentieth century.

3

Margaret Thatcher
Britain's Iron Lady

*M*argaret Thatcher took great pride in her reputation as the Iron Lady. "Any leader has to have a certain amount of steel in them," she said matter-of-factly. "What is the good of having a leader who cannot make up his or her mind, never knows what to do, hems and haws . . . ? He might be a very nice person, but not a leader."

Although the blunt-talking, conservative-minded prime minister was nicknamed the "Iron Lady" for her firm stand against Communism, the title stuck because of her firmness on just about everything. As prime minister of the United Kingdom of Great Britain (England, Scotland, and Wales) and Northern Ireland—four countries united by one government commonly called Britain or the U.K.—Margaret Thatcher set out in 1979 to make Britain great again.

Once the center of a vast and wealthy empire, Britain had fallen on hard times after World War II. German bombs had destroyed much of London, and the cost of the war effort had left the British economy in ruins. To put Britain back on its feet, the government took over various industries and social services. Thatcher deplored this "welfare state" and vowed to replace it with the enterprising values of her youth: hard work, competition, and self-reliance.

Born Margaret Hilda Roberts on October 13, 1925, in Grantham, England, the future prime minister was the daughter of Alfred Roberts, a grocer, and Beatrice Stephenson Roberts, a seamstress before her marriage. Margaret's early life revolved around school, the Methodist church, and home "over the shop."

Margaret adored her father, a hard-working, public-spirited man who served on the Grantham town council for 25 years and as mayor for one term from 1945 to 1946. "Never do things or want to do things just because other people do them," he once told her. "Make up your own mind about what you are going to do and persuade people to go your way." Margaret worked hard to follow her father's advice.

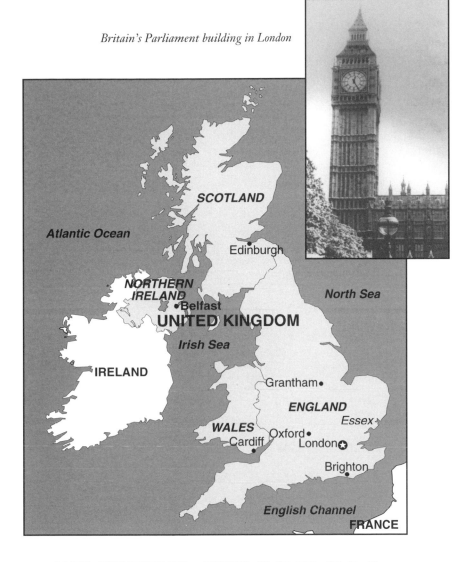

Britain's Parliament building in London

UNITED KINGDOM

Capital: London
Area: 94,475 square miles
Population: 57,890,000
Languages: English, Welsh, Gaelic
Religion: Protestant majority; Roman Catholic, Jewish, Muslim, and Hindu minorities

Voting Age: All citizens age 18 and over
Currency: Pound Sterling
Gross Domestic Product Per Person: $19,500
Literacy Rate: 99%
Life Expectancy: 79 female, 73 male

Margaret remembered her mother, Beatrice, as being "weighed down by the home, always being in the home." But Beatrice passed on to her daughter "the ability to organize and combine so many different duties of an active life."

At the age of 10, Margaret won a poetry reading contest at her school. The headmistress congratulated her on her luck. "I wasn't lucky," Margaret replied with characteristic self-confidence. "I deserved it."

Margaret went on to prestigious Oxford University, where she majored in chemistry and became president of the school's Conservative Association. After graduating in 1947, Margaret worked as a research chemist for a plastics company in Essex. Politics, though, was her passion.

In Britain, Parliament is the main law-making body, consisting of the House of Lords and the House of Commons. Members of the Lords are not elected by the people. The majority of members inherit the right to sit in Parliament along with a family title, such as earl or duchess.

The real legislative power resides in the House of Commons, to which members of Parliament, or MPs, are elected. There are two major political parties in Britain, Labour and Conservative, also called Tory. The MPs in each party elect one of their members to be party leader. Whichever party receives the most votes in an election is in power, and the leader of that party becomes prime minister, the political head of state.

Candidates for office need not live in the district they are representing. Leaders of political parties choose whom they want to run for office in each district. In the 1950 election, the Conservative Party picked Margaret Roberts to challenge what was considered a "safe" seat for the Labour Party in the town of Dartford, north of London. Her chances of winning were slim.

Conservative Party candidate Margaret Roberts (left) campaigned hard to represent the people of Dartford.

At the age of 24, Margaret Roberts was the youngest woman candidate on record. She lost the election but impressed Conservative Party leaders with her speaking ability and her grasp of the issues. In 1951, she ran again and lost once again, but this time by a smaller margin.

During her 1950 campaign, Margaret met Denis Thatcher, a divorced businessman 10 years her senior. The friendship blossomed, and the couple married in 1951. Denis was interested in politics, but he was content to stay in the background. Margaret enrolled in law school. In 1953, she gave birth to twins, a girl and a boy, Carol and Mark. Four months later, she qualified as a *barrister*, a British lawyer allowed to argue cases in higher courts. After hiring a nanny for the twins, Margaret Thatcher went to work, specializing in tax and patent law.

In 1959, Thatcher finally got what she wanted most: a chance to run for a safe Conservative seat in the House of Commons. She easily won election to represent affluent Finchley, a section of north London.

As a newcomer in the House of Commons, Thatcher joined the other "backbenchers," or junior members, assigned to the back of the room. She spoke confidently without notes, peppering her speeches with well-chosen facts and statistics. Praised by her colleagues as a quick learner, she made steady progress up the parliamentary ladder of power.

In 1962, Conservative prime minister Harold MacMillan promoted Thatcher to a front-bench position as parliamentary secretary of the ministry of pensions and national insurance. MacMillan may have chosen her as a "token" woman to replace the woman who had previously held the post. Because women were a rarity in the House of Commons, they generally received more publicity than men. And Thatcher did well in the limelight because she was a skilled debater.

In 1964, the Conservative Party lost its majority in the House of Commons. Thatcher, however, remained in Parliament. The Conservatives regained their majority in 1970 under Edward Heath, a man Thatcher admired. Unlike previous Conservative candidates who had gone along with the Labour Party's proposals for enlarging the government's role in society, Heath proclaimed his aversion to big government in his campaign slogan, "Stand on Your Own Feet."

Unlike presidents in the United States who can name anyone to be a cabinet head, prime ministers choose their cabinet members from among their party's members of Parliament. Heath appointed Margaret Thatcher as his minister of education. She began work trimming the education budget, partly by eliminating free milk for older students. She wanted to use the savings to fund a primary-school building program. The opposition, however, viewed the cut as an attack on essential services and denounced her as "Maggie Thatcher, the Milk Snatcher."

In 1972, Heath made a political about-face and increased the control of government to bolster the

Prime Minister Edward Heath with Elizabeth II, who was proclaimed queen of the United Kingdom in 1952

economy. The measures, though, had little positive effect on the fuel crisis and runaway inflation gripping the nation.

In February 1974, the Labour Party swept the Conservatives out of power with support from powerful labor unions, also called trade unions. Edward Heath was still head of the Conservative Party, and organized his "shadow cabinet," a group of advisers who would be moved into real cabinet positions if the party returned to power. Although he named Thatcher shadow minister of environment, she was becoming disenchanted with his leadership.

When Heath announced elections for party leader, Thatcher declared herself a candidate against her one-time mentor. Bookmakers in gambling parlors gave her only a 50-to-1 chance of winning the February 1975 election. But, surprisingly, she beat Heath by 130 to 119 in the first round of balloting. He resigned in humiliation. "I will always be fond of dear Ted," Thatcher commented, "but there is no room for sympathy in politics."

Over the weekend, Margaret Thatcher told the Young Conservatives Conference that Britain needed "to back the workers, and not the shirkers." The next week, she won the final balloting for party leader, 146 to 79, becoming, at age 49, the first woman to lead one of Britain's major political parties.

During the winter of 1978 to 1979, the so-called "winter of discontent," public service workers staged a series of strikes for higher wages that crippled the everyday lives of millions of people. Garbage piled up on the streets. Schools and hospitals shut down. Gravediggers refused to bury the dead. Britain seemed on the verge of economic collapse.

Describing the situation during the strikes as a return to "barbarism," Thatcher proposed a motion in the House of Commons calling for a vote of "no confidence" in the government. In Britain, parliament is dissolved and new general elections are held if a majority of

Newly elected as head of the Conservative Party, Margaret Thatcher celebrated with her husband, Denis (right), and their son, Mark.

members of the House of Commons vote "no confidence" in the party in power. On March 28, 1979, after a heated debate that lasted for seven hours, Thatcher's motion passed by a mere one vote—311 to 310. Parliament was dissolved and a general election scheduled for May.

Now a candidate for prime minister, Thatcher promised to end Britain's "slither and slide" toward welfare-state socialism by reducing government regulation, cutting taxes, and limiting the power of the trade unions. The Conservative Party won a solid victory, beating

Labour by 43 seats in the House of Commons. Conservative Party leader Margaret Thatcher became the first female prime minister in the history of Britain.

After Thatcher won the May 1979 election, Queen Elizabeth II summoned her to Buckingham Palace and made her victory official by requesting that she form a new government. Like the wives of countless previous prime ministers, husband Denis waited downstairs in the palace while Margaret had her audience with the queen.

The United Kingdom is a constitutional monarchy. The ruling king or queen is head of state and presides over important ceremonies, such as opening or dissolving Parliament. The monarch may reject a bill passed by Parliament, but none have done so since the early 1700s. It is the prime minister who governs.

New prime minister Margaret Thatcher forged ahead with a program to strengthen the economy. The government began selling off state-owned companies, including British Telecom, British Air, and Rolls Royce, to workers and the general public. Public housing, too, became private. The percentage of adults living in their own homes increased from 52 to 66 percent. Thatcher cut the basic rate of income taxes from 33 percent to 25 percent and the top rate from 83 percent to 40 percent, allowing individuals to keep more of their earnings.

Not all British citizens, however, benefited from her new economic program, or "Thatcherism," as it was called. Unemployment doubled between 1979 and 1980 when many businesses went bankrupt due to lack of government support. In 1981, high unemployment aggravated racial tensions. Riots broke out in more than 30 British cities and towns and in 20 London neighborhoods.

Some critics accused Margaret Thatcher of being cold and uncaring. Never one to be slowed by criticism, she tossed off objections to her leadership style as typical male chauvinism. "When a woman is strong, she is strident," Thatcher declared. "If a man is strong, gosh, he's a good guy."

At the same time, Thatcher irritated feminists by failing to name a single woman to her cabinet and refusing to speak out on women's rights. "You just say there are certain human rights that are available to both men and women," she said. "But I don't think men and women can necessarily be the same."

Yet even Thatcher's critics were in awe of her strong will and daunting stamina. Able to get by on five hours of sleep a night, she stayed up until early morning poring over her papers. She was a bold, innovative leader who wanted nothing less than to change "the soul" of the British people. A woman of principle, she once said, "I am not a consensus politician. I'm a conviction politician. The reason I am in politics is because I believe in certain things and try to put them into practice."

In 1982, the prime minister responded with characteristic firmness to Argentina's invasion of the Falkland Islands, a tiny group of islands near the tip of South

America. British farmers and shepherds had settled there in the 1600s. Although other countries had laid claim to the islands, British rule was established on the Falklands in 1833. When asked to choose, the 2,000 islanders preferred to remain loyal to Britain. Thatcher insisted that Argentina's aggression would not be tolerated, that the country could not take by force what it had failed to win through persuasion.

Dismissing calls for her resignation by members of Parliament who faulted her for failing to prevent the invasion, she quickly sent a fleet of 98 ships carrying 8,000

British citizens bid farewell to one of the many ships Margaret Thatcher dispatched to recapture the Falkland Islands from Argentina.

fighting men to take back the Falklands. Seventy-four days later, Argentina surrendered.

Thatcher's popularity soared. "Britain is great again," she declared. Buoyed by their victory, the British people seemed to forget about their economic woes. Thatcher scheduled elections for June 9, 1983. When the votes were tallied up, the Conservatives won again with a majority of 141 seats over the combined opposition parties, Labour and Social Democratic/Liberal Alliance.

Thatcher began her second term with inflation down and the power of the unions significantly curbed. By replacing the old show of hands with the secret ballot, the Thatcher government made it illegal for union leaders to bully their members into voting to strike.

In March 1984, Arthur Scargill, president of the National Union of Mineworkers, called a strike to protest government plans to cut coal production by 4 percent. The strike was an illegal one, as Scargill had failed to get a vote from union members. About 40,000 of the 180,000 miners continued to work during the strike, lessening its effectiveness. A year later, Scargill called off the strike, and miners drifted back to work. Ironically, the strikers had given the Coal Board just what it wanted—a drop in coal production.

In the midst of the coal strike, Thatcher attended the Conservative Party conference in Brighton. During the early morning hours of October 12, 1984, a bomb ripped through one section of the Grand Hotel near

Thatcher's suite. The window of her sitting room blew out into the street as she sat up late reading reports. Four people were killed in the blast; a fifth person died later from her injuries. Margaret Thatcher spoke at the conference the following morning as scheduled, telling the audience that "all attempts to destroy democracy by terrorism will fail."

The Irish Republican Army (IRA), an outlawed terrorist organization, claimed responsibility for the bomb. The IRA wanted to end British control of Northern Ireland so it could be united with its predominantly Catholic neighbor to the south, the Republic of Ireland. In 1921, Britain had created separate governments for the mostly Protestant north and the Catholic south, which became the independent Republic of Ireland in 1949. Thatcher and Prime Minister Garret FitzGerald of the Republic of Ireland signed an agreement in 1985 giving Ireland an advisory role in the government of Northern Ireland. But Northern Ireland's Protestants rejected the plan.

Thatcher was more successful in improving relations between the United States and the Soviet Union. Although a long-time opponent of Communism, she had met Soviet president Mikhail Gorbachev in 1984 and instantly empathized with his plans to loosen government control of the Soviet economy and hold elections. Margaret Thatcher helped convince the United States that Gorbachev was sincere and could be trusted.

Thatcher won reelection on June 11, 1987, but her popularity was waning. Advocates for the poor denounced her plans to privatize the National Health Services and blamed her policies for an increase in homelessness. Leaders within her own Conservative party—often called Tories—disagreed with Thatcher's opposition to a common European Monetary System.

Most unpopular of all was Thatcher's new household tax, or poll tax, on all British citizens, which replaced the old system that affected only property owners. The new

Thousands of demonstrators marched past the Parliament building during this 1990 protest against the controversial poll tax.

poll taxes went into effect on April 1, 1990, despite mass protests in London and several other cities.

In late 1990, Thatcher sent a strong military force to the Persian Gulf to help the United States and other countries oppose Iraq's invasion of Kuwait. But as the troops gathered in the Gulf, Thatcher was unable to rally her own Conservative Party. Many members of her government believed she had no chance of winning the next election. Thatcher resigned as party leader on November 22, 1990, but retained her seat in the House of Commons. John Major was elected Conservative Party leader and formed a new government.

British troops fought in the Persian Gulf War in January 1991. Although Iraq's president Saddam Hussein was forced to withdraw his troops from Kuwait, Margaret Thatcher has stated that the failure of the allies "to disarm Saddam Hussein and to follow through the victory . . . was a mistake. Hussein was left with the standing and the means to terrorize his people and foment more trouble."

During her eleven and one-half years as prime minister, Margaret Thatcher reorganized Britain's economic system, skillfully handled international affairs, and rekindled a sense of pride in her nation. In doing so, she changed the course of British history. Her country recognized her many accomplishments in 1995 by granting her the title of baroness. She is now Lady Thatcher.

Corazón Aquino (b. 1933) completed her husband's mission to return democracy to the Philippines and oversaw the passage of a new constitution that limited the power of the president.

4

Corazón Aquino
Yellow Rose of the Philippines

*I*f her husband, Benigno "Ninoy" Aquino Jr., had lived, Corazón Aquino might have remained a self-professed housewife in the Philippines. But when Ninoy was gunned down at the Manila airport on August 21, 1983, the country turned to Cory Aquino to fill her husband's role as the leading opponent to Philippine dictator Ferdinand Marcos.

At first, Aquino refused to run, saying she wanted to stay out of politics. She changed her mind, however, after a million people signed a petition for her candidacy.

In February 1986, thousands of people took to the streets wearing yellow, the color of Aquino's party, in a bloodless revolution of "people power" that restored democracy to the Philippines.

Aquino's political entry was less sudden than it seemed. She had grown up in a prominent political family: Her father, Jose "Pepe" Cojuangco, was a congressman and her grandfather served as a senator. Like many Filipinos, the Cojuangcos were of mixed ancestry—Chinese, Malaysian, and Spanish—reflecting different eras in the country's history.

In 1521, Portuguese navigator Ferdinand Magellan, funded by the king of Spain, landed in the Philippines, a chain of more than 7,000 islands located in the Pacific Ocean off the coast of Southeast Asia. Twenty-one years later, Spanish explorer Lopez de Villalobos named the islands for the young prince who later became King Philip II of Spain. During the next three centuries, the Spanish converted most of the natives to Roman Catholicism.

In 1898, the United States won the Philippines as part of the settlement of the Spanish-American War. During World War II, from 1942 through 1944, the Japanese occupied the entire country. Finally, on July 4, 1946, the United States granted the Philippines its independence. The new nation adopted a constitution and a system of government similar to that of the United States.

Yet, for all its Americanization, the Philippines of Aquino's youth still clung to an old feudal order. A few

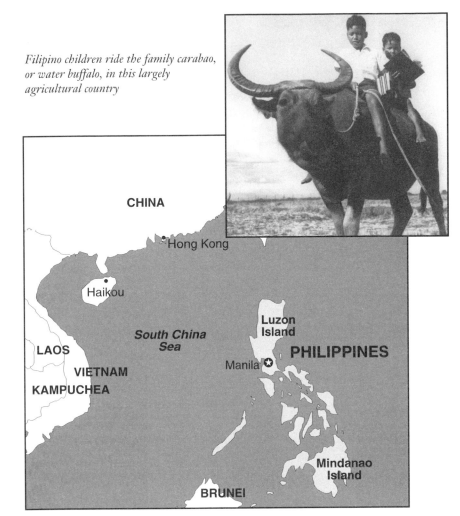

Filipino children ride the family carabao, or water buffalo, in this largely agricultural country

CHINA

Hong Kong

Haikou

LAOS

VIETNAM

KAMPUCHEA

South China Sea

Luzon Island

PHILIPPINES

Manila

Mindanao Island

BRUNEI

PHILIPPINES

Capital: Manila
Area: 115,800 square miles
Population: 76,103,000
Languages: Tagalog, English, Spanish
Religion: 83% Roman Catholic, 9% Protestant, 5% Muslim

Voting Age: All citizens age 15 and over
Currency: Philippine peso
Gross Domestic Product Per Person: $2,530
Literacy Rate: 94%
Life Expectancy: 67 female, 63 male

rich families—including Corazón's—ruled the land. Corazón's father, Jose Cojuangco, owned a vast sugarcane plantation, and her mother, Demetria Sumulong, held a bachelor's degree in pharmacy. Born María Corazón Cojuangco on January 25, 1933, Cory, as she was called, attended elite Catholic schools in Manila, graduating first in her class. Despite their great wealth, the Cojuangcos lived simply. Demetria taught her children the values of thrift, punctuality, and self-discipline. Cory wore hand-me-downs from her sisters and learned to hide her strong will behind a soft voice and good manners.

In 1946, 13-year-old Cory and her family left the war-torn Philippines for the United States. Cory attended Roman Catholic convent schools in Philadelphia and New York City and then the College of Mount St. Vincent, a small Catholic women's college in New York, where she majored in French. Cory was also fluent in four other languages—Spanish, English, Japanese, and Tagalog, the native language of the Philippines.

Upon returning to the Philippines to study law at Far Eastern University in 1953, Cory began seeing Benigno "Ninoy" Aquino Jr., an up-and-coming journalist from a wealthy family in Manila. Their fathers were friends. Ninoy proposed, but at first Cory turned him down, saying she wasn't ready for marriage.

Finally, Cory agreed to marry Ninoy, leaving school after just one semester. Their wedding on October 11, 1954, paired not only two powerful Filipino families but also two distinctly different personalities: Ninoy's boisterous sociability and Cory's calm reserve.

Ninoy plunged headfirst into politics while Cory stayed at home to tend to their growing family. The couple had five children—four girls and one boy. The gregarious Ninoy brought home a steady stream of friends and supporters, expecting his wife to serve as his hostess.

Ninoy quickly shot up the political ranks. He was elected mayor of Concepcion—a small town where he owned a farm—then governor, and then senator, all by the age of 34. He might have become the youngest president in the Philippines had he not been thrown in jail in 1972 for his political opposition to Ferdinand Marcos.

Elected president of the Philippines in 1965, Marcos had initially won over the people by promising to make the nation great again. Yet he failed to make good on his promise. As economic setbacks and social unrest threatened the country, Marcos became more dictatorial. On September 21, 1972, he declared martial law and abolished Congress. He jailed political opponents and controlled the press. In 1973, he forced the ratification of a new constitution that gave the president virtually unlimited power. Marcos credited himself with inventing a new form of government, which he called "smiling martial law."

But just about the only one smiling was Marcos himself. Most Filipinos continued to live in poverty.

Because of his strong stand against Communism, the United States initially supported the presidency of Ferdinand Marcos (1917-1989).

Marcos and his wife, Imelda, on the other hand, lived lavishly, treating the nation's treasury like a personal checking account. They squandered billions of dollars on such extravagancies as the more than 1,000 pairs of shoes Imelda owned. Meanwhile, thousands of political opponents—including Ninoy Aquino—were jailed.

During Ninoy's imprisonment, Cory served as Ninoy's link to the outside world. She delivered messages and called press conferences. When he disappeared, she searched from prison to prison until she found him. During his 40-day hunger strike, she brought him vitamins in a thermos.

In 1980, while still in prison, Ninoy suffered a major heart attack and was granted permission to come to the United States for medical treatment. After successful surgery, he accepted fellowships first at Harvard University and later at the Massachusetts Institute of Technology. His family settled in the affluent Boston suburb of Newton. Cory later described the next three years as the happiest of her life.

While Ninoy served as the social center of the family, Cory supplied the moral backbone. She disapproved of the rough-and-tumble politics Ninoy was willing to play to beat the system. Whenever she walked into a room, all talk of political intrigue ceased.

Ninoy, however, longed to rejoin the political fray. Despite warnings of threats against his life, he insisted on returning to the Philippines. On August 12, 1983, the night before he left, Cory cooked him his favorite meal: Peking duck. That night, Ninoy told a reporter, "This is a second life I can give up. Besides, if they shoot me, they'll make me a hero." His words turned out to be prophetic.

Well-wishers gathered at the Manila airport to welcome Ninoy with yellow ribbons, a symbol of homecoming from the song, "Tie a Yellow Ribbon 'Round the Old Oak Tree." Suddenly, soldiers hustled the former senator off the plane. The journalists and friends who had been traveling with Ninoy waited helplessly as the soldiers prevented them from leaving the plane. Then shots rang out. Ninoy Aquino was dead. A man the government claimed was Aquino's assassin was also killed, but many believed both men were victims of Marcos's soldiers.

Back in Newton, Cory Aquino worried that something was wrong. Unable to sleep, she prayed a report that her husband had been shot was just a rumor. But it wasn't. She and her children packed their bags and returned to the Philippines.

Almost two million Filipinos attended Ninoy's funeral, making it the largest procession in the history of the Philippines. Opposition leaders clamored for Cory Aquino to carry on her husband's work. Finally, on December 3, 1985, the day after top military officers were acquitted of conspiring to murder her husband, Aquino announced her candidacy for president.

"I plan to seek justice not only for Ninoy but for all the victims of Marcos," she said. On the official certificate for candidacy, she listed her occupation as "housewife" but added, "I am not a housewife anymore because I cannot take care of my house anymore."

Her campaign began slowly. Then, throwing away her prepared speeches, she spoke simply as a victim of Marcos's extravagant and dictatorial rule. A heated battle ensued, with Aquino pitting her own strong sense of morality against Marcos's quest for unbridled power.

Cory Aquino's supporters held a rally in Manila only a few days before the February 1986 election.

Marcos found it demeaning to run against a woman. One of his campaign vans blared: "What the country needs is a man! A bull! A stud! Vote Marcos, Marcos!" Marcos's flamboyant wife, Imelda, got into the act, too, chiding Aquino for wearing yellow, a color Imelda found unattractive.

Aquino, in turn, criticized Imelda Marcos for having nothing better to do than talk about her wardrobe in a country in which millions of people were poor and hungry. As for Ferdinand Marcos's accusations of inexperience, she retorted, "Sure, I don't know anything about stealing or cheating, and definitely I don't know anything about killing my opponents."

On February 7, 1986, millions of Filipinos flocked to the polls. In an election marred by widespread cheating, pro-Marcos forces ripped up ballots and intimidated voters at gunpoint. More than 30 people were killed in campaign-related violence.

Both candidates claimed victory, pointing to two different sets of election returns. Calls poured in from around the world denouncing the election fraud. Declaring herself the winner at a huge rally in Manila on February 16, Aquino launched a nonviolent campaign of strikes and boycotts to topple the Marcos government. The Catholic Church threw its support firmly behind her. Cory Aquino declared that she would accept nothing less than Marcos's removal from office.

Then two of Marcos's top military officers, Defense Minister Juan Ponce Enrile and General Fidel Ramos, defected to join forces with Aquino. Hundreds, then thousands, then tens of thousands of ordinary citizens took to the streets for four days of nonviolent revolution. The protesters gave flowers to Marcos's soldiers surrounding the compound where Enrile and Ramos had taken refuge, and they knelt before the tanks, praying the rosary. Unwilling to shoot these peaceful protesters,

Marcos's men withdrew. In a modern version of David and Goliath, the small woman in yellow led supporters bearing only flags and flowers against Marcos's military.

On February 25, 1986, U.S. president Ronald Reagan called for Marcos to resign. Under cover of night, Ferdinand and Imelda Marcos quietly fled the Philippines, bound for Hawaii.

Aquino believed that her gender had made a difference. "Women are less liable to resort to violence than men," she later said in a *Time* interview, "and at this time in my country's history, what is really needed is a man or woman of peace."

Aquino soon learned that winning was easier than governing this poor, politically divided country. Many Filipinos had unrealistically high expectations and looked to her to cure decades of poverty, corruption, and disorganization overnight. Communist rebels clashed with the Filipino army.

"You people were so tolerant and so patient under Marcos for 20 years," she said, "and here I am only two days in office and you are expecting miracles." Making good on her campaign promises, Cory Aquino released more than 500 political prisoners, appointed a commission to draft a new constitution, and turned the opulent presidential palace into a museum. For the first time, Philippine citizens could see examples of the lavish way the Marcos had lived, including Imelda's 888 handbags and 71 pairs of sunglasses.

Imelda Marcos (b. 1930), shown here in a 1966 visit to the United States, lived luxuriously while the majority of Filipinos languished in poverty.

On September 15, 1986, despite rumors of a military coup, Aquino set out for Washington to raise funds to help her nation pay off its debts. In honor of her visit, many members of the U.S. Congress pinned yellow rosebuds to their lapels or donned yellow ties. Aquino told the legislators about her country's return to democracy and received a standing ovation for her moving account.

Congress voted to give the Philippines $200 million in emergency aid.

Upon returning home, Aquino stumped for a new constitution. A vote for the constitution would, in effect, be a vote for her, for it would grant her an automatic six-year term of office. On February 2, 1987, 80 percent of the eligible Filipino voters—22 million—went to the polls. They overwhelmingly approved the American-style constitution, with 76 percent voting in favor of it.

As in the United States, the Filipino government has three branches. The president and vice-president, elected to six-year terms, and the president's cabinet make up the executive branch. Congress, the legislative branch, has both a senate and a house of representatives. The 24 senators serve for six years and are elected by the entire country. About 200 representatives are elected to serve specific districts for three-year terms. Another 50 are appointed by the political parties to ensure that women and minorities are adequately represented. A supreme court makes up the judicial branch of the government.

Aquino brought a new openness to government. Cultivating a "softer," more inclusive style than that of her predecessors, she appointed several women to executive positions. But she combined gentleness with tenacity. U.S. representative Stephen Solarz called her a "woman who has a steel fist inside a velvet glove."

In 1988, the United States charged Ferdinand Marcos with improperly using money from the Philippines to buy

In August 1986, Cory Aquino (center) visited her husband's hometown of Concepcion where a brass statue of Benigno Aquino was erected. Also shown are (from left) Benigno's mother, Aurora Aquino; son Noynoy; and daughters Kris and Balsy.

American real estate. Marcos, however, became seriously ill, and the charges were dropped. He died in 1989.

Marcos's old supporters in the Philippines, meanwhile, conspired to overthrow the Aquino government. On seven separate occasions, disgruntled members of the military attempted to seize power. The most serious coup attempt came in December 1989. If not for the military intervention of the United States, Cory Aquino might not have remained in power. After nearly a week of fighting, 100 Filipinos, mostly civilians, were dead. The Aquino administration was badly shaken, and President Aquino's once phenomenal popularity was fading.

Each coup attempt hurt the economy, sending a message of political instability to foreign investors. As these investors pulled out, unemployment rose. Cory Aquino's supporters blamed the economic problems on the former Marcos regime. Distracted by conspiracies, Aquino had little time to focus on economic reform. She had, however, reduced the foreign debt as well as the threat of Communist insurgency.

In 1990, Aquino formed her own political movement called Kabisig, meaning "linked arms" in Tagalog. Its purpose was to inspire citizens to jolt the sluggish legislature into making positive changes. Critics, however, faulted the movement for being "too little, too late."

The following year, Aquino lobbied the Philippine Senate to renew the leases of the U.S. military bases. Some 85,000 Filipinos were employed either directly or indirectly by the U.S. military. In a burst of Philippine nationalism, the senators rejected the president's advice. Among the senators who voted against the continued U.S. military presence was the president's own brother-in-law, Senator Agapito Aquino. "We need to cut the apron strings with America, even though we are scared to do it," he stated.

The Philippine Senate also blocked Aquino's attempts at land reform. While some protesters criticized her for failing to turn her family's plantation over to its workers, more conservative critics accused the president of being weak and indecisive.

"The problem with some of our people is that they would like to have the best of both worlds," Aquino complained. "They would like me to have some dictatorial powers, with everybody else living under a democracy."

Rejecting all pleas to run again, Aquino threw her support behind her former defense minister, Fidel Ramos, in the May 1992 election. She turned over her office to Ramos, the victor in the seven-way race, in a peaceful transfer of power that contrasted sharply with the violent transitions of the past.

Cory Aquino retired to private life, confident that she had given the job her all. Besides reestablishing democracy, she had drawn up a new constitution and created a new, more open style of government. She planned to work for voluntary organizations in her new found free time.

"I always made a joke of having restored democracy and freedom for the Filipino people but losing it for me in the process," she said upon leaving office in 1993. "But now I've gained it back."

*During the 1992 election, Corazón Aquino supported
her former defense secretary, Fidel Ramos (left), to
succeed her as president. He won the seven-way race.*

"I am a daughter of the East, educated in the West,"
former Pakistani prime minister Benazir Bhutto
(b. 1953) described herself. "I see myself as a bridge
between two worlds, two pasts."

5

Benazir Bhutto
Pakistan's Price of Democracy

*B*enazir Bhutto rose to power in a Muslim country in which women were not even encouraged to work outside the home, much less to become prime minister. She inherited the leadership of the political party begun by her father, Pakistani prime minister Zulfikar Ali Bhutto, who was ousted by the military in 1977 and hanged two years later.

When military rule eventually gave way to free elections, the charismatic 35-year-old, in 1988, became the first female Muslim prime minister as well as the youngest elected leader in the world at that time. But her triumph did not last long. Under a military-era amendment to the constitution, Bhutto was dismissed on charges of corruption, reelected, and dismissed again. Even her own mother turned against her. "Sometimes I look at all the different stages of my life and think it reads like fiction," Benazir Bhutto observed in 1994.

Benazir grew up in a country steeped in drama. Ruled by the British during the 1800s and early 1900s as a part of India, Pakistan became an independent nation in 1947. A year earlier, Britain had offered to grant India independence once the people agreed on a form of government. But the Hindus leading the independence movement in India clashed with the minority Muslims who wanted a nation of their own. Unlike their Hindu neighbors who believe in many deities and regard the cow as sacred, Muslims worship only one God, Allah, and generally eat beef. Many Muslim women live in *purdah*, isolated at home and heavily veiled in public.

The disputed region was partitioned into two separate countries, India and Pakistan (meaning "Land of the Pure" in the Urdu language). During Benazir's youth, Pakistan consisted of two separate sections under one government—East Pakistan and West Pakistan—separated over 1,000 miles by India. The two sections were also divided by differences in language and culture. The division would eventually lead to civil war, and only West Pakistan remains as Pakistan.

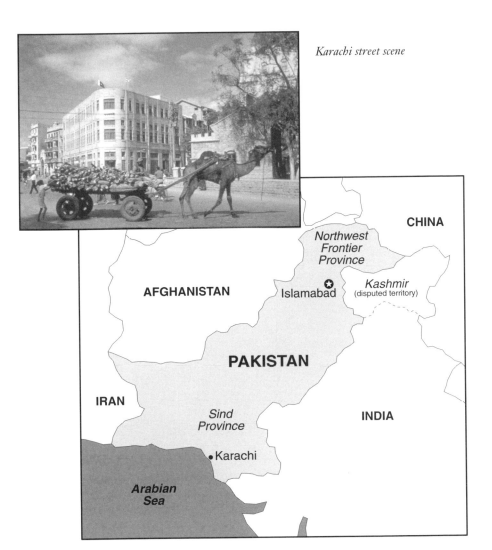

Karachi street scene

PAKISTAN

Capital: Islamabad
Area: 310,320 square miles
Population: 132,185,000
Languages: Urdu, Punjabi, Sindhi, Pushtu, English
Religion: 97% Muslim

Voting Age: All citizens age 21 and over
Currency: Pakistani rupee
Gross Domestic Product Per Person: $2,100
Literacy rate: 37%
Life Expectancy: 59 (female and male)

Benazir Bhutto was born on June 21, 1953, to Zulfikar Ali Bhutto, who served in various cabinet posts before becoming head of state, and his second wife, Nusrat Ispahani Bhutto, an Iranian. As a 13-year-old boy, Zulfikar Ali had agreed to marry one of his cousins to keep the Bhutto lands within the family. He and his first wife never lived together, and they saw each other only at family gatherings. Since Pakistani men were allowed to have four wives, he decided to marry again.

Nusrat was a nontraditional Muslim woman who defied custom by tooling around the streets of Karachi in her own sports car. She and Zulfikar Ali parted ways with traditional Muslims by refusing to separate the females from the males in their household. The Western-educated Zulfikar Ali wanted his daughters to have the same opportunities as his sons.

Benazir, whose name means "matchless," was her father's favorite. She, in turn, idolized him. As the eldest of four children—two boys and two girls—she was often left in charge of the household along with the family servants while her parents traveled. This responsibility helped to hone her leadership skills at an early age.

One day, Nusrat Bhutto introduced her 12-year-old daughter to the *burqa*, the black tent-like veil traditionally worn by Muslim women in public. Benazir, however, hated the way the veil sealed in the heat and turned her world gray. Her father decided she didn't need to wear it. "Let her be judged by her character and her mind, not her clothing," Zulfikar Ali Bhutto said, thus freeing his young daughter from what she would later call "a life spent in perpetual twilight."

In autumn 1969, 16-year-old Benazir traveled to America to attend Radcliffe College. At first, she was shocked by the easy mixing between male and female students. But she came to regard her time at Radcliffe as "a true awakening" that sharpened her faith in democracy.

In 1970, Pakistanis elected a National Assembly that was to draft a new constitution. (Military leaders controlled the government during the late 1950s and 1960s.) A majority of members came from the more populous East Pakistan, and they wanted the constitution to grant them more self-government. In response, President Yahya Khan postponed the first meeting of the National Assembly, and angry protests broke out in East Pakistan. When Khan sent the army to quell the rebellion, civil war erupted.

In early December 1971, India threw its support to East Pakistan. Fighting spread into the province of Kashmir, on the Indian and West Pakistan border. (Kashmir remains disputed territory.) More than a million people died in the fighting before West Pakistan surrendered two weeks later. East Pakistan became the independent new nation of Bangladesh. In West Pakistan, the military regime gave up its power and elections were held. Zulfikar Ali Bhutto and his Pakistani People's Party (PPP) won and headed up what remained of Pakistan.

Educated at the University of California-Berkeley and at Oxford in England, Zulfikar Ali Bhutto (1928-1979) served as his country's minister of commerce (1958) and foreign minister (1963) before his election as prime minister in 1971.

In June 1972, Benazir accompanied her father to a summit meeting with Prime Minister Indira Gandhi of India. Benazir later wrote that Gandhi kept staring at her. Perhaps Gandhi was remembering that as a young woman, she, too, had accompanied her statesman father to meetings with other heads of state.

The following year, Zulfikar Ali Bhutto brought his daughter to the White House, where she struck up a conversation with Secretary of State Henry Kissinger. After dinner, Kissinger told Bhutto, "Mr. Prime Minister, your daughter is even more intimidating than you are."

Smiling with pride, Zulfikar Ali put his arm around his daughter's shoulders and said, "She's a fighter, like me."

Benazir graduated cum laude from Radcliffe in the spring of 1973 with a degree in government. She then went to graduate school at Oxford University in England, where she became the first foreign woman elected to head the Oxford Union, the university's prestigious debating society. Her father had also held this post when he studied at Oxford.

In 1973, a new Pakistani constitution was approved that provided for a parliament consisting of a national assembly and a senate with a president as head of state and a prime minister as chief executive. Bhutto resigned as president to become prime minister. In 1977, he won reelection, but reports that he had tampered with the election results led to widespread rioting. Although Zulfikar Ali Bhutto espoused democratic principles, he resorted to authoritarian rule, outlawing opposition parties and jailing their leaders.

In June 1977, Benazir Bhutto completed her studies at Oxford and returned to Pakistan, much to the delight of her father. Just 10 days later, on July 5, the military seized control of the government, imprisoning Zulfikar Ali Bhutto and installing army chief of staff, General Mohammed Zia ul-Haq, as head of state.

Benazir Bhutto's two brothers, Murtaza and Shahnawaz, who were studying abroad, were warned not to return home. On April 3, 1979, Benazir Bhutto and

After fighting in World War II, Mohammed Zia ul-Haq (1924-1988) rose through the army ranks to become general and army chief-of-staff in 1976.

her mother, who were also imprisoned at the time, visited her father in prison for one last time. "You don't know how much I love you, how much I've always loved you," he told her. "You are my jewel."

The following day, Zulfikar Ali Bhutto was hanged and his body secretly taken to the family's estate in Larkana and buried in a family plot. Benazir Bhutto spent the next seven years in and out of prison and house arrest. Her two brothers, meanwhile, formed Al-Zulfikar, a terrorist organization based in Afghanistan. In early 1981,

94

the group hijacked a Pakistani International Airlines plane to Syria to force General Zia to release some imprisoned Bhutto supporters in exchange for the passengers.

Zia released the supporters but arrested thousands of other political opponents—Bhutto and her mother among them. This time, imprisonment for Bhutto meant solitary confinement in a filthy, insect-infested prison. The heat in her cell reached 120 degrees. Bhutto's hair fell out in clumps, and her skin split and peeled. A doctor who treated her for an ear infection pierced her eardrum, leaving her deaf in one ear. In December 1981, she was released from prison but placed under house arrest. Her ear again became painfully infected.

Finally, an old Harvard friend, Peter Galbraith, who was working for the U.S. Senate Foreign Relations Committee, intervened on Bhutto's behalf. In January 1984, she received permission to travel to Britain for ear surgery. She received a warm welcome in London, and her release was widely covered by the media.

Benazir Bhutto's nerves were frayed from her years of imprisonment and isolation. Yet, as head of the PPP abroad, she wanted her followers to see her as strong, so she learned to hide her fears and calm herself by taking deep breaths. She was committed to restoring civilian rule in Pakistan.

Zia, meanwhile, swept away Zulfikar Ali's democratic reforms and imposed strict Islamic rule. Religious minorities were terrorized. Alcohol and gambling were banned. Crimes such as theft were punished by flogging or cutting off the convicted person's hand. A woman's testimony was legally worth only half as much as a man's.

In July 1985, Bhutto flew to Cannes, a resort village in the French Riviera, for a family reunion that was marred by the death of her youngest brother, Shahnawaz. Bhutto believed that Shah was poisoned out of fear that he would resume his guerrilla attacks on the Zia regime. At great risk to her own safety, she returned to Pakistan with her brother's coffin. The funeral turned into a massive antigovernment rally.

Back in London, Bhutto received word that Zia had lifted martial law. On April 10, 1986, she returned to Pakistan to huge, cheering crowds, vowing to carry on her father's mission and sacrifice everything for her country. Bhutto embarked on a tour of Pakistan, winning over crowds with her dramatic speeches. Pointing to the recent triumphs of democracy in the Philippines and in Haiti, she told Pakistanis that 1986 was "a bad year for dictators" and that "now another dictator must go."

Then Bhutto was again arrested and placed in solitary confinement. Upon being freed a month later, she was threatened by a number of attempts on her life. To throw her enemies off track, she often made three different plans for one trip.

Being a single woman also presented problems. She could not live by herself because single women in a Muslim society traditionally live with another family member. Although she wanted to marry and have children, dating was out of the question. Any hint of a relationship between Bhutto and a man could be used by her political opponents to destroy her. Finally, she agreed to an arranged marriage to Asif Ali Zardari.

Like Bhutto, Zardari came from a powerful land-owning family in Sind. Shortly after they met, Bhutto was stung by a bee, and her hand became swollen. Zardari insisted on taking her to see a doctor. Touched by this act of caring, she married him in December 1987.

Instead of taking her husband's name, Bhutto kept her own. Zardari agreed to look after any children and to allow his wife to go to prison for her beliefs. "You must agree that Benazir will serve the nation," Bhutto's family said. "This is all right with me," he replied, "for I will serve the nation by serving my wife."

In May 1988, Zia unexpectedly dissolved Parliament and called for elections, but he died in a plane crash that summer. Bhutto interrupted her campaign for the upcoming election to give birth to her first child, a boy named Bilawal, on September 21, 1988. Five days later, she was again campaigning. The PPP won the November 16 election. As party leader, on December 1, 1988, Benazir Bhutto became the first woman prime minister of Pakistan.

Once elected, Bhutto faced the even more formidable task of governing her troubled nation. Three out of every four Pakistani citizens were illiterate, and millions lacked proper shelter, schools, hospitals, even drinking water. After 11 years of military rule, Pakistanis looked to Bhutto as their savior, greeting her with joyous shouts of "Jiye Bhutto!" ("Bhutto Lives!").

Benazir Bhutto promised to improve the lives of her people, but she spent much of her time feuding with the political opposition, especially Nawaz Sharif. Unlike the United States, Pakistan had no clear separation between church and state. The Islamic Democratic Alliance, headed by Sharif, wanted to make Muslim religious dictates the civil law of the land.

Bhutto faced other problems as well. Women's rights activists complained that she wasn't doing enough to curb the power of Islamic fundamentalists. Charges of corruption in her government filled the papers almost daily. Cabinet seats, for example, were bartered for increased support for her policies in Parliament. Bhutto also lacked the support of military holdovers from the old regime.

On August 6, 1990, President Ghulam Ishaq Khan evoked a Zia-era provision to dismiss Bhutto as prime minister. Bhutto's husband was charged with corruption but was later released for lack of conclusive evidence. New elections brought Bhutto's nemesis, Nawaz Sharif, to power. As head of the PPP, Bhutto assumed the role of parliamentary opposition leader.

Eager to make a political comeback, Bhutto turned to British prime minister Margaret Thatcher for advice. Thatcher advised her to remain above the fray while her two rivals attacked each other. The strategy worked. In 1993, Khan dismissed Sharif on charges of corruption. New elections were called for October 1993, and Bhutto's PPP scored a narrow victory.

Much to Bhutto's dismay, however, her brother, Murtaza Bhutto, returned from exile abroad to challenge her right to inherit their father's political legacy. Nusrat

Nusrat Bhutto and Murtaza Bhutto at a press conference in 1995

Bhutto backed her son instead of her daughter, proclaiming that the family's "male line" were her late husband's true heirs. When Nusrat and her supporters went to visit Zulfikar Ali's grave, Benazir called out the national police to turn them away. Nusrat angrily compared her daughter to General Zia, saying, "She talks a lot about democracy, but she's become a little dictator."

At the outset of her second term, Bhutto vowed to adopt a tougher stance. "This time, I won't listen to the sloppy liberals," she said, implying that Pakistan needed to be governed differently from a Western-style democracy. Instead of heeding America's call for Pakistan to discontinue its nuclear program, Benazir Bhutto defended it as a necessary protection against India. No longer did Bhutto believe she could stay in office without the political support of the military. In keeping with the vindictive traditions of Pakistani politics, she transferred or demoted judges, reporters, and officials who angered her.

While Bhutto continued to dazzle Western admirers with her populist oratory, citizens in her homeland complained that she had gone back on her democratic promises. She spoke eloquently about women's rights but failed to change the Pakistani laws that denied those rights. She spoke about improving the lives of the poor but supported privileges for the landholding elite.

Pakistan was teetering on the brink of political chaos. The Northwest Frontier Province became one of the world's primary sources of illegal narcotic drugs. In

Karachi, rival ethnic groups took to the streets with guns. The violence claimed at least 1,200 lives. Among them were two United States government workers gunned down in a U.S. Embassy van. A third American was wounded in the attack.

Turning to the United States for help, Bhutto won $12.3 billion in aid to fight terrorism and drug trafficking. She worked tirelessly to attract foreign investment and won passage of new drug laws extending the death penalty to drug traffickers.

Supporters credited Bhutto with keeping democracy alive, no matter how fragile, for the longest single period in her country's history. "She's ruling in a jungle, and it's not easy," declared Asma Jahagir, chairman of the human rights commission of Pakistan.

Bhutto's husband, however, was widely disliked. A polo-playing businessman, Zardari was popularly known as "Mr. Ten Percent" for the portion of government contracts he allegedly kept for himself as minister of investments. On September 20, 1996, Bhutto's estranged brother, Murtaza, was killed in a shoot-out with police, and Zardari was jailed on charges of involvement in the killing. The prime minister stood by her husband, convinced of his innocence. Pleading for his release from prison, she insisted he had been framed for the killing.

Benazir Bhutto's own support, though, was also waning. In autumn 1996, Islamic fundamentalists in the military tried unsuccessfully to overthrow the

*Asif Ali Zardari holding his daughter Asifa, one of
the three children he and Benazir Bhutto have had
since their arranged marriage in 1987. "I decided to
make a personal sacrifice in what I thought would be
a loveless marriage," recalled Benazir. "The
surprising part is that we are very close and that it's
been a very good match."*

government. Shortly after the attempted coup, Pakistan's president Farooq Leghari, a longtime Bhutto supporter, dismissed her as prime minister on November 5, 1996, on charges of corruption. Bhutto angrily blamed Leghari for having "driven the knife into the heart" of Pakistani democracy.

In new elections held on February 3, 1997, Nawaz Sharif's Pakistan Muslim League won 136 seats in the 207-seat National Assembly. Voter turnout was barely 30 percent, reflecting the public's distrust of politicians.

Soon after Bhutto left office, investigators in Pakistan uncovered evidence of high-level corruption in her administration. A front-page story in the January 9, 1998, *New York Times* stated that Pakistani investigators traced more than $100 million to foreign bank accounts controlled by Bhutto's family. They discovered that many foreign companies had made deposits to these accounts, allegedly in exchange for business favors. Although Bhutto's name did not appear on any documents uncovered, evidence suggested that her husband had received payoffs and was involved in illegal deals.

Currently chair of the PPP, Bhutto described the investigation as persecution. In a speech given in April 1998, in Minneapolis, Minnesota, she stated, "For the past 18 months my party, my family, and myself have been persecuted. My husband languishes in prison—a hostage to my political career." Her children live in an undisclosed country to protect their safety.

A wife and mother turned publisher and politician, Violeta Barrios de Chamorro (b.1929) ended a civil war in Nicaragua when she was elected president in 1990.

6

Violeta Barrios de Chamorro
Nicaragua's Peacemaker

*T*hroughout Nicaragua's civil war in the 1980s, Violeta Barrios de Chamorro kept the peace in her own family. Two of her children backed the leftist Sandinistas, while the other two sided with the opposition. But Chamorro declared political discussion off-limits in her home when everyone gathered for Sunday dinner.

"The Sandinistas have tried to split families, to divide them psychologically, mentally, in their ideology," she explained. "But I think that, deep inside, it is very difficult for those divisions to last."

In 1990, Chamorro, the widow of crusading newspaper publisher Pedro Joaquin Chamorro Cardenal, became the first female president of Nicaragua. Applying the peacemaking lessons she learned as a mother to her position as head of state, she ended the long civil war that had claimed some 30,000 lives.

Nicaragua has a long history of political differences. In 1502, Christopher Columbus claimed the country for the Spanish throne on his fourth and final trip to the New World. Named for the native Nicarao Indians, Nicaragua won its independence from Spain in 1821. A series of strong-arm presidents, backed by feuding political factions, ruled the land, with one group always trying to overpower the other. One faction's hero was another group's villain.

Nicaragua's past is closely linked to that of the United States. William Walker, an American adventurer, declared himself president of Nicaragua in July 1856, but he was defeated the following year. In 1911, U.S. banks began to lend money to Nicaragua in exchange for allowing American businesses to operate there. Some Nicaraguans opposed the American presence in their country. In 1912, the United States dispatched the marines to Nicaragua to quell the unrest. They would remain for more than 20 years.

From 1927 until his death in 1934, General Augusto Cesar Sandino led attacks against the U.S. Marines from hideouts in the mountains. The United States trained a

Augusto Cesar Sandino (1895-1934), shown here in 1929, led guerrilla resistance to U.S. occupation forces. He was honored as a hero and a martyr by many Nicaraguans after his death.

new Nicaraguan army, the National Guard, and Anastasio Somoza Garcia became its head. In 1934, the United States left Nicaragua, and Somoza ordered his forces to assassinate Sandino. Three years later, Somoza became dictator of Nicaragua. Many Nicaraguans in the following decades, including Violeta and Pedro Chamorro, would consider Sandino to be a national hero.

When Pedro Chamorro, the son of a newspaper publisher, met 19-year-old Violeta Barrios, he fell in love at first sight. During one of his visits, Violeta suggested they play cards. She won every time. Unlike the girls in the capital city of Managua who were in awe of his position and prominent family, Violeta could hold her own, and Pedro respected her.

Born on October 18, 1929, in Rivas, Violeta Barrios Torres grew up one of seven children of a wealthy cattle rancher, Carlos Barrios Sacasa and his wife, Amalita Torres de Barrios. (With Spanish names, it is customary to use a double surname: first, the father's family name—his father's name—second, the mother's surname—her father's name. The second surname is often dropped in everyday usage. If a woman marries, she generally drops her mother's family name and adds *de* and her husband's first last name to her father's name. She would usually be referred to by her husband's last name.)

An athletic and musical child, Violeta attended private Catholic boarding schools. When she went off to high school, her father advised her: "Never discuss politics or religion, and you will see you will get along with everyone." At her father's urging, Violeta then enrolled at a private women's college in the United States, Blackstone College in Virginia, but she never quite mastered the English language. She returned home after one year because her father died. As the eldest daughter, she was responsible for helping her mother run the household.

In 1950, Violeta married Pedro Chamorro. After his father died in 1952, Pedro ran his family's newspaper, *La Prensa* (The Press). Passionate about politics, Chamorro used the paper to oppose Somoza, who controlled the economy in Nicaragua and smothered all political dissent against his government.

After an unsuccessful coup against Anastasio Somoza in 1956, Chamorro was arrested and imprisoned for rebellion, and then banished to an isolated village called San Carlos. Pedro and Violeta escaped by boat across the

Idealistic newspaper publisher Pedro Joaquin Chamorro was frequently jailed during the 1950s for opposing the Somoza government.

southern border into Costa Rica, where their four children were allowed to join them. Later that same year, Somoza was shot by an assassin. But his rule continued through his sons, Luis Somoza Debayle, president from 1957 until 1963, and Anastasio Somoza Debayle, who assumed power in 1967.

In 1960, the Chamorros returned to Nicaragua when the government offered exiles and dissidents *amnesty*, a general pardon for political offenses. Pedro again took charge of *La Prensa*, and resumed his attacks on the Somozas, which resulted in his serving time in prison. During this time, Violeta Chamorro saw her role as simply that of a wife and mother.

Pedro Chamorro, however, viewed his wife as the carrier of his torch. Convinced that he might be killed, he spoke to her about the responsibilities she would inherit upon his death. She protested that she did not want them, that she wanted to die before him.

But she did not get her wish. On January 10, 1978, Pedro was driving to *La Prensa* when another car forced him off the road. Assassins then shot and killed him. Violeta heard the news in Miami, Florida, where she and her daughter, Cristiana, were shopping for Cristiana's wedding trousseau. Most Nicaraguans blamed the killing on the Somoza regime.

The murder of Chamorro unleashed decades of frustration and anger with the dictatorial rule of the Somozas. An estimated 50,000 people followed Pedro

Chamorro's coffin to the cemetery. His brother, Jaime, said the murder "ignited the national insurrection against Somoza" which was fought by the guerrilla army known as the Sandinista National Liberation Front (named for the martyred Sandino). After 18 months of civil war, Anastasio Somoza Debayle fled the country for Paraguay. Two days later, on July 19, 1979, the Sandinistas marched triumphantly into Managua.

Violeta Chamorro initially supported the Sandinista cause and contributed $50,000. But, after agreeing to serve on a five-member governing council called a *junta*, she became disenchanted with the new government's intolerance of differing points of view.

Although chosen for the council because of her husband's work and her own moderate stance, Chamorro found herself overpowered and outmaneuvered by the more radical members of the group. After nine months, Chamorro resigned, officially citing health reasons, but privately accusing the Sandinistas of losing interest in promoting democracy.

In 1984, Sandinista leader Daniel Ortega Saavedra was elected president. Ortega nationalized private property and industry in order to narrow the gap between the rich and the poor. He appointed a number of women to prominent positions, including Chamorro's daughter, Claudia, who became ambassador to Costa Rica. Ortega, however, also forbade any political dissent. He was a virtual dictator.

Chamorro took over the reins of *La Prensa* and before long was attacking the new government. As the premier voice of opposition, *La Prensa* began receiving aid from the United States and other nations. American-backed guerrilla soldiers known as Contras, short for counter-revolutionaries, waged a war against the Sandinista regime from bases across the northern border in Honduras. The United States became involved because the Communist countries of Cuba and the Soviet Union were assisting the Sandinistas. The civil war between the Sandinistas and the Contras escalated throughout the 1980s.

Like many families in war-torn Nicaragua, Chamorro's was becoming polarized. Her oldest daughter, Claudia, and youngest son, Carlos Fernando, served in prominent positions in the Sandinista government, but her son Pedro Joaquin and daughter Cristiana opposed the Sandinistas.

In June 1986, the Sandinista government closed down *La Prensa* for attempting "to justify United States aggression." The presses remained silent for 15 months. The Central American peace accord, signed by the presidents of Costa Rica, Guatemala, Honduras, and El Salvador, and Chamorro's refusal to publish a censored paper, prodded Ortega to allow the newspaper to reopen, uncensored. The peace accord had little other effect until 1989, when the Central American presidents persuaded Ortega to hold free elections on February 25, 1990.

On October 1, 1987, Violeta Chamorro held up a copy of the first issue of La Prensa *published in over a year, pointing to the photograph of her murdered husband, Pedro. The headline read "The people triumph*—La Prensa *without censorship."*

Anti-Sandinista groups then began looking for someone capable of uniting the factious opposition and defeating Ortega. As the mother of two Sandinistas and two anti-Sandinistas and the widow of an opponent to the Somozas, Chamorro emerged as the only candidate capable of uniting the 14-party *Union Nacional Opositora* (UNO), or National Opposition Union. Although a

113

political novice, Chamorro benefited from the expertise of anti-Sandinista intellectuals and politicians who had spent two years hammering out a party platform that called for, among other things, restoring private enterprise and ending the unpopular military draft. The Sandinistas recruited young people off the streets and forced them to fight with little or no military training.

In a country known for its culture of *machismo*, the idea that men must be extremely aggressive, virile, and brave, many doubted that Violeta Chamorro would have the strength, stamina, and will to endure a rigorous political campaign. Chamorro, however, flourished on the campaign trail. Being a woman turned out to be a strength rather than a weakness. She served as a symbol: the sacrificing mother of a divided nation.

Early in the campaign, Chamorro fell and broke her kneecap. Confined to a wheelchair, she rode in the back of a pickup truck under a white canopy, paraded around like a patron saint displayed at festival time. Dressed in white and wearing a simple gold crucifix, she was introduced at political rallies as "the white dove of peace."

During the campaign, Chamorro addressed crowds tired of the political dogma of the Sandinistas. She often talked about restoring traditional values to strengthen the family. Delivering an emotional plea for reconciliation, Chamorro spoke in broad terms about her opposition to the military draft and her plans for peace. Admittedly inexperienced in politics, she sometimes forgot the names

A broken leg did not prevent candidate Violeta Chamorro from reaching voters throughout Nicaragua. She usually rode in the back of a pickup truck, shaded by a canopy. This stop was in Villa Carlos Fonseca, 25 miles southwest of Managua.

of prominent heads of state and referred questions about economic reform and foreign policy to her advisers.

The Sandinistas—including Chamorro's own son, Carlos Fernando, editor of the official Sandinista newspaper, *Barricada* (Barricade)—accused the UNO of being a puppet of the old Somoza dictatorship, the United States, and the American-backed Contras. Several leaders

115

of the UNO campaign, including Chamorro's other son, Pedro Joaquin, were, indeed, former Contra leaders, and the United States Congress had contributed $9 million in aid toward the Nicaraguan election. But most of the American money went to the government commission administering the vote. None of the funds the UNO received could be used for campaigning.

On election day, February 25, 1990, Chamorro won 55 percent of the vote to Ortega's 41 percent. When Daniel Ortega hesitated to admit defeat, former United States president Jimmy Carter convinced him to concede.

Daniel Ortega at a press conference three days before he lost the presidential election to Violeta Chamorro.

Carter was one of several hundred international observers who had come to Nicaragua to ensure a fair election and that the votes were accurately counted. The next morning, Ortega congratulated Chamorro on her victory. She joined him in urging the Contras to lay down their arms. On April 19, 1990, the rival groups signed a ceasefire. By June, the Contras had disbanded.

At her inauguration six days later, Violeta Chamorro declared, "Reconciliation is more beautiful than victory." In a move to placate the Sandinistas, she announced her decision to retain Humberto Ortega Saavedra, the former president's brother, as head of the military. Two of her new cabinet appointees resigned in protest, but Chamorro explained, "Without his [Humberto Ortega's] cooperation it would have been virtually impossible to depoliticize and shrink the army peacefully."

Chamorro soon found herself under fire from both sides of the political spectrum. Liberals in the legislature, which was called the National Assembly, faulted her for dismantling state economic controls. Conservatives, on the other hand, complained that property was being returned too slowly to its private owners. And feminists criticized Chamorro for her close ties to the Catholic Church as well as for her failure to promote women's rights. Then a rash of strikes paralyzed the nation, scaring away private investors. With the economy in shambles, fighting broke out in the countryside between the remobilized Contras and the Sandinistas.

To add to the problems, relations between Chamorro and the old UNO coalition broke down over the continuing influence of the Sandinistas—Humberto Ortega, in particular—and allegations of corruption. One administration official accused of corruption fled to Bolivia, then blamed the wrongdoing on Chamorro's son-in-law, Antonio Lacayo Oyanguren, the minister of the presidency.

Known by some as the "de facto president," Lacayo was widely considered the most powerful person in Nicaragua. Lacayo came under fire for his strict policies, which reduced inflation but failed to promote economic growth. Chamorro, though, stood by her son-in-law. "If Antonio goes, Violeta goes," she declared in 1992.

Doña Violeta, as she was called, remained personally beloved by Nicaraguans. She was devout and motherly, calling her ministers and advisers "my love." Supporters said her uncanny common sense more than made up for her lack of political experience.

Nevertheless, problems persisted. By early 1993, Violeta Chamorro's political coalition had officially withdrawn its support. With two-thirds of the work force unemployed, old political tensions flared between the Sandinistas and the Contras.

In August 1993, pro-Contra rebels kidnapped 38 legislators, soldiers, and government officials and then demanded the dismissal of Humberto Ortega and Antonio Lacayo. Pro-Sandinistas retaliated by kidnapping 34

Scarlet macaw: one of several species of tropical birds found in Nicaragua

NICARAGUA

Capital: Managua
Area: 57,130 square miles
Population: 4,386,000
Language: Spanish
Religion: 95% Roman Catholic
Voting Age: All citizens age 16 and over

Currency: Cordoba
Gross Domestic Product Per Person: $1,700
Literacy Rate: 65%
Life Expectancy: 68 female, 63 male

UNO members, including Vice-President Virgilio Godoy Reyes, and calling for the release of the first group of hostages. No one was injured during the week-long crisis, which ended when all hostages were freed unharmed and both sides agreed to an eight-point plan to alleviate tensions.

In February 1995, Humberto Ortega stepped down as defense minister. But his departure failed to satisfy Chamorro's opponents in the National Assembly. That summer, relations deteriorated between her and the National Assembly over proposed constitutional reforms.

The National Assembly had revised the 1987 constitution to limit the power of the presidency. Close relatives, such as Antonio Lacayo, would be prohibited from running for president. Chamorro argued that the legislature did not have the power to approve such drastic changes. After a four-week battle with the National Assembly, Violeta Chamorro backed down and agreed to a new constitution on June 15, 1995. Lacayo resigned less than two months later, on September 7, 1995.

The country, meanwhile, remained the second poorest in the Western Hemisphere, behind only Haiti. Much of the property confiscated by the Sandinistas had yet to be returned to its former owners. Although economic problems persisted, Nicaraguans were slowly developing tolerance for each other's differences. In her six years in office, Chamorro had subordinated military power to civilian rule and had restored peace.

On February 7, 1996, Pope John Paul II visited Nicaragua. After Chamorro embraced the pope, she apologized to him, explaining that in Nicaragua emotions sometimes got in the way of protocol. Instead of being offended, the pope was clearly pleased by her warmth. He waved his aides aside and tightly held her hand. President Chamorro asked what John Paul thought of the nation of Nicaragua. When he praised the progress toward peace, Chamorro exclaimed, "Thank you, thank you, Holy Father. My dreams have come true."

Chamorro chose not to run for reelection in 1996. Former president Daniel Ortega ran for office once again, this time trying to shed his radical past and asking forgiveness for the mistakes of his Sandinista regime. The people of Nicaragua, however, voted instead for Arnoldo Aleman, the conservative former mayor of Managua.

Violeta Chamorro's autobiography, *Dreams of the Heart*, was published in 1996. In early 1997, she left office, planning to launch an educational foundation to help less privileged citizens become future leaders of the nation. In *Dreams of the Heart*, she wrote, "we must substitute our culture of confrontation with one of tolerance and a love for peace."

In Norway, a land of majestic mountains and narrow inlets of sea called fjords, nearly every citizen excels in at least one outdoor sport. Gro Harlem Brundtland (b. 1939), who describes herself as "absolutely typically Norwegian," has skied the 25-mile trip from her house to her mountain cottage.

7

Gro Harlem Brundtland
Green Goddess of Norway

*M*uch as her Viking ancestors set sail to conquer new lands, Gro Harlem Brundtland ventured beyond her native Norway to explore new political frontiers.

Along the way, the three-time prime minister became known around the world as a feminist and an environmentalist. When she took office for the second time in May 1986, she appointed 8 women to her 18-member cabinet—the highest percentage of women in top government posts in the world. Brundtland gained world recognition, too, as the chairwoman of the United

Nations World Commission on Environment and Development, which published its landmark report, "Our Common Future," in 1987.

Norway has long been a trailblazer in social reform and women's rights. During the Viking period, around A.D. 1000, Norway's legal system made no distinction between men and women. Gender equality was a necessity, as women took charge of the farms and governed the fishing villages when the men were away at sea.

In 1913, Norway became the second country in Europe to extend voting rights to women. (Finland was the first.) In 1966, the nation's one-house parliament, the Storting, passed a sweeping social welfare program, encompassing benefits such as health insurance, aid for mothers and orphans, job retraining, and retirement pensions. In 1978, Norway passed the Equal Status Act prohibiting sexual discrimination. This small, prosperous, racially homogeneous nation has long boasted one of the highest standards of living in the world. While few Norwegians are extraordinarily rich, few are extraordinarily poor.

Born Gro (pronounced Grew) Harlem on April 20, 1939, in Oslo, Norway, the future prime minister grew up in a politically committed family. Both her parents were active in Norway's Labour Party, which was founded in 1887 to champion workers' rights. Her father, Gudmund Harlem, a medical doctor, was a minister in the Labour Party government and personal physician to several prime

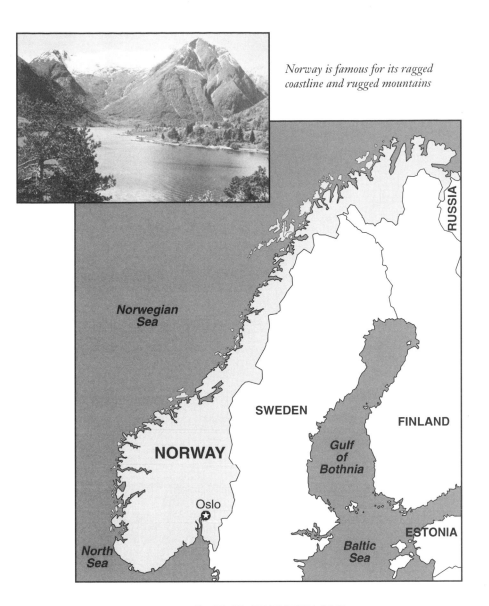

Norway is famous for its ragged coastline and rugged mountains

NORWAY

Capital: Oslo
Area: 149,412 square miles
Population: 4,399,000
Languages: Norwegian (Bokmal and Nynorsk), Lapp
Religion: 87% Christian (Lutheran)

Voting Age: All citizens age 18 and over
Currency: Norwegian krone
Gross Domestic Product Per Person: $24,500
Literacy Rate: 99%
Life Expectancy: 81 female, 74 male

ministers. Her mother, Inga Harlem, also worked for the Labour Party.

During World War II, when Gro was just two years old, the family left Nazi-occupied Norway for Sweden, where her father served with Norway's anti-Nazi resistance. Back in Oslo after the war, Gro joined the Labour Party's children's group when she was seven years old. At the family dinner table, she was always the one asking why the government could not do more to help its citizens. Her heroes included Joan of Arc and Golda Meir.

Gro Harlem grew up in an atmosphere that assumed equality between the sexes. She played sports with the boys but also developed a feminine side. When she decided she wanted to have both a medical career and a family, no one tried to change her mind. She studied medicine at the University of Oslo, where she served as vice-chair of the Socialist Student's Association, a branch of the Labour Party.

In 1960, Gro married Arne Olav Brundtland, a political scientist. From the start, they shared household responsibilities. She nursed the first of their four children—three boys and a girl—between classes at medical school. When Arne Olav got his degree the following year, he took over responsibility for taking the baby to daycare in the morning and picking him up in the afternoon.

Upon graduating from medical school in 1963, Gro Harlem Brundtland attended Harvard University's School of Public Health. There, through her studies of pollution problems, she became interested in environmental protection. She returned to Oslo in 1965 and served as a consultant to the Ministry of Health and Social Affairs.

Brundtland's political work soon eclipsed her medical career, although she saw clear connections between the two. "The doctor first tries to prevent illness, then tries to treat it if it comes," she said. "It's exactly the same as what you try to do as a politician, but with regard to society."

In September 1974, Prime Minister Trygve Bratteli appointed Brundtland minister of environmental affairs. When she told her husband about the appointment, he agreed to take over the bulk of the domestic responsibilities as long as he could do them his way. In their hallway, he hung a sign saying "A House Must Be Clean Enough to be Healthy and Dirty Enough to be Happy."

Gro Harlem Brundtland believed that men needed to participate more fully in household matters in order for women to achieve equality in the workplace. She knew from personal experience that women needed help at home in order to pursue a political career.

As she saw it, men and women brought different strengths to their positions. "A natural balance of men and women makes prejudiced decisions less likely and provides the greatest possible breadth of experience," she observed. Women, she said, were more apt than men to back up their political thinking with personal examples and observations.

Gro Harlem Brundtland's tenure as environmental minister coincided with the rising awareness of ecological issues around the world. Dubbed the "Green Goddess," she developed a popular system of nature preserves and worked to protect the environment from the dangers of offshore drilling.

Meanwhile, the Labour Party, to which she was elected vice-chairman in 1975, was floundering. Four years later, in 1979, Brundtland left her post as environmental secretary to devote her attention to revitalizing the party. Opinion polls indicated that the Labour Party would lose to the Conservatives in the September 1981 election.

In January 1981, Prime Minister Odvar Nordli resigned as leader of the Labour Party. Officially, he stepped down for health reasons, but political insiders attributed Nordli's resignation to the party's dissatisfaction with his leadership. On February 3, 1981, the Labour Party's central committee unanimously elected Gro Harlem Brundtland to take over as prime minister, and she formally took office the following day.

At 41, Brundtland became the youngest person— and the first woman—ever to serve as prime minister of Norway. She won praise for her self-assured style, organizational abilities, and sense of optimism. But critics complained that the new prime minister was too direct and aggressive. While supporters lauded her keen intellect, detractors complained about her fiery temper.

"It was very tough in 1981," Brundtland said about her first brief tenure as prime minister. "In the worst of times I always thought, 'If you can get through this, it will be much better for the next woman.'"

Brundtland grappled with the nation's rising inflation by freezing prices. Conservatives, on the other hand, advocated a different approach: cutting taxes and scaling back the government bureaucracy. Norway was being swept up in the rising tide of conservatism affecting both Europe and the United States. On September 13 and

14, 1981, voters elected a right-wing coalition headed by Kare Willoch, an advocate of supply-side economics and an admirer of U.S. president Ronald Reagan.

In 1983, Gro Harlem Brundtland was asked to head the United Nations World Commission on Environment and Development. Brundtland and her commission spent the next three years gathering scientific data and holding public hearings in all parts of the world. Concerned that average people be heard on the issues, she opened up the hearings to ordinary citizens as well as scientific experts. Brundtland juggled her leadership of the commission with her responsibilities in Norway. Still head of the Labour Party, she presided over the the passage of a 1983 rule requiring that 40 percent of all Labour candidates for public office be women.

As the 1986 election approached, Gro Harlem Brundtland campaigned hard for the Labour Party. Opponents used her husband's membership in the Conservative Party against her. "Do As Gro Did," declared one campaign poster. "Choose a Conservative." "Do as Arne Olav did," Brundtland countered. "Choose Gro."

The Norwegian people followed her advice. In May 1986, Brundtland embarked on her second term as prime minister. Since women had made such rapid advances in the political arena, she had no trouble finding 8 qualified women to serve in her 18-member cabinet. Thirty-four percent of the members of Norway's 157-seat Storting were now women.

130

Gro Harlem Brundtland (fourth from the right) with some of her new cabinet members, eight of whom were women, after winning the 1986 election and forming a new government. The women hold red roses, the symbol of the Labour Party.

True to her campaign promises, Brundtland short-ened the workweek to 37.5 hours and extended paid maternity leave to 24 weeks. She capped wages and deval-ued the Krone, the basic unit of Norwegian currency, to restore financial stability.

Meanwhile, Brundtland's work for the United Nations was gaining recognition. In April 1987, the World Commission on Environment and Development released its conclusions. The report, "Our Common Future," revolutionized the field of environmentalism by presenting economic development as a friend rather than a foe of environmental protection. Influential and well received, a special version of the report, *Preserving Our World: A Consumer's Guide to the Brundtland Report*, was published in 1990.

Echoing Indira Gandhi's claim that poverty was the greatest threat to the environment, the report maintained that "the poor and the hungry destroy their own environment . . . in efforts to stay alive." Industrialized countries, on the other hand, tend to squander resources. Developing and industrialized countries are linked together in a vicious cycle. Typically, the cycle begins with developing nations turning to industrialized nations for help. To pay back high-interest loans, however, the developing countries are forced to overcultivate their land, thus triggering more famine and misery. As an alternative to wasting environmental resources, the Brundtland Report called for a program of "sustainable development," which would serve the economic needs of people without damaging the earth or depleting resources.

The report recalled the practice used in medieval times of villagers setting aside common pastures so everyone could share this resource as well as the responsibility to care for it. The report stated, "Today that 'common' spans the globe. . . . If we share the concern and the responsibility, we may also live to share the hope and the rewards." The report called for a sweeping reorganization of the world's priorities. Nationalism needed to give way to internationalism, war to peace. Population growth must be curbed. "The most effective means of family planning is adult, female literacy," the report concluded, advocating better educational opportunities for women.

Even in a highly literate nation such as Norway, women struggled to keep pace with their male counterparts. A 1987 report titled "Scenario 2000," commissioned by a Norwegian research institute, stated that women's gains in the political arena had occurred partly because men were shunning public office for the higher-paying private sector. Although women were becoming more visible in Norwegian politics, they were not yet powerful players in the business world.

Brundtland acknowledged that women had not made significant gains in the private sector, but she disputed the report's conclusion that women were being "marginalized" in government. She said that female politicians were forcing government to put a greater emphasis on key issues, such as child care and education.

In 1989, a coalition led by the Conservative Party won control of the Storting, but Brundtland retained her seat. Then the Conservative coalition, led by Jan Syse, collapsed in 1990, and the Labour Party regained control

Arne Olav (left front) and Gro Harlem Brundtland picnicking with their sons, Knut, Ivar, and Jörgen; daughter Kaja; and a friend

of the government. Brundtland began her third term as prime minister—a particularly triumphant one for women's rights.

In 1990, the Storting amended its constitution to allow women to inherit the throne. Norway is a constitutional monarchy like the United Kingdom but, prior to 1990, only men could serve as monarch. By 1991, 59 of the 165 members of the Storting were women.

Yet while Gro Brundtland won raves from feminists, she encountered criticism from some environmentalists over whale hunting. In 1992, Norway broke a seven-year international moratorium on commercial whaling. This, some environmentalists said, amounted to "pirate whaling." Brundtland replied that the population of minke whales had grown so plentiful they could now be hunted in accordance with her notion of sustainable development. Decisions about whaling should be based on scientific evidence rather than sentiment, she said.

That same year, Brundtland stepped down temporarily from office. Sadly, one of her three sons, 24-year-old Jörgen, had committed suicide in September.

Upon resuming her responsibilities in 1993, Brundtland encouraged Norwegian diplomats involved in secret negotiations to bring peace to the Middle East. The months of meetings near Oslo resulted in a historic peace agreement between Israel and the Palestine Liberation Organization (PLO), the Oslo Accord.

In the September 13, 1993, election, the Labour Party faced challenges from two parties, Center and Conservative, also led by women. Brundtland, a symbol of women's achievement in Norway, once again retained her position as prime minister.

In autumn 1994, Gro Harlem Brundtland's recommendation that Norway join the European Union clashed with the isolationism of many Norwegians. The question of whether to remain separate from or join with other countries had long been a divisive one. Norway's distrust of outsiders was rooted in its history of domination by other countries. In 1536, Norway was overpowered by Denmark; then, in 1814, by Sweden. The word "union," used by the Swedish colonialists, gave the name European Union a negative meaning to many Norwegians.

Brundtland, however, believed that membership in the union would give Norway an economic boost and enhance its national security. But, in the 1994 elections held on November 28 and 29, Norwegians rejected union by a vote of 52.2 percent to 47.8 percent.

Despite this rejection, Norway's economic forecast looked rosy due to its increased production of natural gas. Eighty-five percent of the revenues were expected to stay within the country, thus protecting its high standard of living for years to come. A promise of cooperation on trade and environmental matters from Russian president Boris Yeltsin in March 1996 added to the country's sense of optimism.

In October 1996, Gro Brundtland resigned as prime minister. Labour Party leader Thorbjoern Jagland took over as prime minister on October 25, 1996, pledging to keep women in at least 40 percent of his cabinet positions. Brundtland also decided not to seek another term in the Storting when her term ended in October 1997.

Her contributions, though, remain. Feminists around the world point to Norway as a success story—a nation in which women are integrated into the political

Gro Harlem Brundtland added another first to her list of accomplishments when she was appointed the first woman director-general of the World Health Organization (WHO) in 1998. An agency of the United Nations, WHO researches world health problems and promotes high medical standards.

system, thanks largely to the efforts of Brundtland. Environmentalists, too, credit her with contributing not only to her native Norway but also to the world at large. Brundtland's view of economic development changed the thinking of people around the world.

"Suddenly there was hope that we could turn back the tide of pollution smothering the world," wrote journalist Warner Troyer in his introduction to *Preserving Our World.* "Suddenly everyone was quoting from the Brundtland Report."

Edith Cresson of France (top left), Kim Campbell of Canada (top right), and Jenny Shipley of New Zealand

8

More Women Leaders

*U*ntil the twentieth century, the only way a woman could govern her country was to inherit the throne. The rise of feminism and democracy have opened up new doors for women—and they have been walking through those doors in ever increasing numbers. In addition to the seven leaders profiled in this book, there have been other women who led their nations.

Sirimavo Bandaranaike (b. 1916), prime minister of Sri Lanka. In 1960, Sirimavo Bandaranaike, the widow of assassinated Prime Minister Solomon Bandaranaike, became the first female prime minister in the world. Although she had no previous political experience, she was elected with the understanding that she would continue her late husband's Socialist policies. But worsening economic conditions and ethnic unrest led to her party's loss of power in 1965. In 1970, Bandaranaike returned to office for a troubled second term. Food shortages beset the South Asian island, and the minority Tamil population agitated for a separate state. In 1977, Sirimavo's Freedom Party was swept out of power.

Mary Eugenia Charles (b. 1919), prime minister of Dominica. The granddaughter of former slaves, Mary Eugenia Charles studied law at the London School of Economics and Political Science. Then she returned home to become the first female lawyer in Dominica, a small Caribbean island that was a British possession at the time. Charles cofounded the Dominica Freedom Party, which helped gain independence for the nation in 1978. Upon becoming prime minister in 1980, she implemented economic reforms and curbed corruption. In 1983, she helped to persuade U.S. president Ronald Reagan to invade Grenada to protect it from Cuban domination. Charles encouraged tourism but remained adamant about preserving the ecology and national identity of the island. When asked about women's rights, she replied, "In Dominica, we really live women's lib. We don't have to expound it." Mary Eugenia Charles resigned in 1995 after 15 years in office.

Vigdís Finnbogadóttir (b. 1930), president of Iceland. Presidents of this island country act as symbols of national unity and as cultural ambassadors, not as political heads of state. A former French and drama teacher and theater director, her background served her well in this post. First

Dominica prime minister Mary Eugenia Charles conferred with U.S. president Ronald Reagan about Grenada in 1983.

elected in 1980, President Vigdís, as she was known, won reelection three times, holding office until 1996.

Maria Liberia-Peters (b. 1941) became prime minister of the Netherlands Antilles in 1984. This country consists of two groups of islands in the West Indies and is part of the Kingdom of the Netherlands. Educated in Europe, Liberia-Peters was a teacher before entering politics. Her first term lasted two years. She was reelected in 1988 and led her nation until 1994.

Wilma Mankiller (b. 1944), chief of the Cherokee Nation in the United States. The daughter of a Dutch mother and a Cherokee father, Wilma grew up in a family with 10 brothers and sisters. When their Oklahoma farm failed, the Mankillers resettled in San Francisco as part of a federal program to move American Indians from rural towns to urban areas. There Mankiller married and and raised two daughters, but she longed to return to her American Indian roots. After her divorce in 1974, Mankiller returned home to Oklahoma, completed her college degree, and became economic coordinator for the Cherokee Nation. Elected the first female chief of the Cherokee Nation in 1984, Mankiller founded the Cherokee Nation's chamber of commerce and the Institute for Cherokee Literacy. She served as chief for 10 years. In 1998, she was awarded the Congressional Medal of Freedom, the highest civilian honor in the U.S.

Kazimiera Prunskiene (b. 1943), became prime minister of Lithuania in 1990, six days after the Lithuanian parliament had voted for independence from the former Soviet Union. She urged free-market economic reforms and negotiated with Russia to recognize her country's new status. Although she failed on both counts and resigned in January 1991, the Russian government recognized Lithuanian independence nine months later.

Mary Robinson (b. 1945), president of the Republic of Ireland. The daughter of Catholic doctors, Robinson became Trinity College's youngest law professor at the age of 25. As a member of the Senate, she worked for and received a mandate to extend the hand of friendship to British-controlled Northern Ireland. When Robinson ran for president in 1990, Dublin bookmakers listed her as a 1,000-to-1 underdog. Nevertheless, she embarked on a six-month grassroots bus tour and won the election. Working around the constraints of her largely ceremonial office, Mary Robinson found ways to support equal rights for women and convinced many world leaders to support investment in Ireland. In 1997, she chose not to seek reelection. Robinson, who became the United Nations Human Rights Commissioner after she left office, was succeeded by another woman, Mary McAleese.

Edith Cresson (b. 1934), prime minister of France. Chosen to head France's troubled Socialist Party, Cresson became the first female prime minister of France in May 1991. Some viewed the blunt-spoken Cresson as a liberal version of Britain's Margaret Thatcher, whom she admired. But Cresson's gaffs, such as comparing Japanese people to ants, cost her popularity, as did discontent with the Socialist Party because of high unemployment. She resigned in April 1992, less than one year after forming a government.

Khaleda Zia (b. 1945), prime minister of Bangladesh. Khaleda married an army officer, Zia-ur Rahman, when she was 15. Her husband rose through the ranks. He was elected president in 1979, but was assassinated in May 1981. Three years later, when Khaleda Zia took over the leadership of the political party her husband had founded, the Bangladesh Nationalist Party (BNP), she worked to end martial law and restore democracy. When free elections were finally held in 1991, the BNP won, and she became prime minister. Zia focused her efforts on population control and literacy. She was succeeded by another woman and her principal political rival, Awami League leader Hasina Wazed, in 1996.

Hanna Suchocka (b. 1946), prime minister of Poland. Both pharmacists, Suchocka's parents hoped that she would join them in the family business. But Suchocka chose law instead. When Poland first held free elections in 1989, Suchocka was elected to Parliament and then, in 1992, was asked to be prime minister. She believed strongly in the free-market reforms that took place in her country in the 1990s. While the reforms led to economic growth, they also increased unemployment, causing Suchocka's party to lose power in 1993.

Kim Campbell (b. 1947), prime minister of Canada. Like France's Cresson, Campbell held office briefly in an attempt to rescue a troubled political party. Campbell served as justice minister (1990) and minister of defense (1993) before the Progressive Conservative Party chose her to replace resigning Prime Minister Brian Mulroney. She was sworn in as prime minister on June 25, 1993. At the time, Canada was struggling to recover from a three-year economic recession. French separatists in the province of Quebec, who wanted an independent country, presented her with another difficult problem. Campbell's term in office was extraordinarily short—only about four months— as the Progressive Conservatives suffered a stunning defeat in the general election in October 1993. After Campbell lost, she returned to her work as a college professor.

Tansu Ciller (b. 1946), prime minister of Turkey. The daughter of a wealthy provincial governor, Ciller earned a Ph.D. in economics at the University of Connecticut.

Returning to Turkey in 1974, she taught economics before becoming Turkey's economics minister in 1991. Two years later, Ciller was selected to head the True Path Party and she subsequently became prime minister. Her government collapsed in a corruption scandal in 1995.

Chandrika Bandaranaike Kumaratunga (b. 1945), president of Sri Lanka. Kumaratunga continued the legacy left by her parents. Having witnessed not only the assassination of her father, Prime Minister Solomon Bandaranaike, but also that of her husband, Vijaya Kumaratunga, a popular film star and politician, Chandrika Kumaratunga ran for office at the request of her mother, Sirimavo Bandaranaike. In the early 1980s, fighting escalated between the majority Sinhalese population and the minority Tamil rebels. Campaigning to end the long and bloody war, Kumaratunga led her People's Alliance Party to victory in August 1994. She restored human rights and developed a plan to satisfy Tamil demands for self-rule by shifting power from the central government to the provinces. She also appointed her mother prime minister, a position that became less powerful than the president's following a 1978 constitutional change.

Jenny Shipley (b. 1952), prime minister of New Zealand. Jenny Shipley earned a reputation as a tough-minded politician by challenging the many social programs legislated by the New Zealand government. As social welfare minister in the early 1990s, she cut welfare payments and health insurance in an effort to decrease government spending. Angry critics burned her in effigy, but Shipley seemed to relish her notoriety. She was sworn in as prime minister on December 8, 1997.

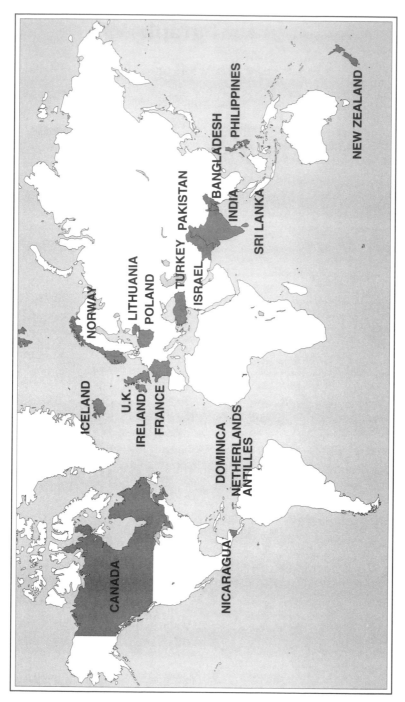

Countries with past or present women leaders

Bibliography

Adams, Faith. *Nicaragua: Struggling with Change.* Minneapolis: Dillon, 1987.

Adler, David A. *Our Golda.* New York: Viking, 1984.

"Aquino, Corazón (Cojuangco)." *Current Biography.* New York: H. W. Wilson, 1986.

Ashby, Ruth, and Deborah Gore Ohrn, eds. *Herstory: Women Who Changed the World.* New York: Viking, 1995.

"Bandaranaike, Sirimavo." *Current Biography.* New York: H. W. Wilson, 1961.

Bennett, Linda. "Meet the Other Women Heads of Nations." *Ms.,* October 1986.

Bhatia, Krishan. *Indira: A Biography of Prime Minister Gandhi.* New York: Praeger, 1974.

Bhutto, Benazir. "Benazir Speaks Her Piece." *World Press Review,* December 1996.

"Bhutto, Benazir." *Current Biography.* New York: H. W. Wilson, 1986.

Bhutto, Benazir. *Daughter of Destiny.* New York: Simon & Schuster, 1989.

———. "The Price of Democracy." Lecture, Minneapolis, April 29, 1998.

Bokhari, Farhan, and Khozem Merchant. "Pakistan's Drift Toward Chaos." *World Press Review,* December 1996.

Bouchard, Elizabeth. *Benazir Bhutto: Prime Minister.* New York: Rosen, 1992.

"Brundtland, Gro Harlem." *Current Biography.* New York: H. W. Wilson, 1981.

Brundtland, Gro Harlem. "Empowering Women." *Environment,* December 1994.

———. "Growth Is Good." *Mother Jones,* April/May 1990.

Burns, John F. "Bhutto Clan Leaves Trail of Corruption." *New York Times,* January 8, 1998.

———. "Pakistan Officials Free a Defiant Bhutto from Custody." *New York Times,* November 7, 1996.

———. "Unveiled Power: A Special Report." *New York Times,* March 29, 1996.

Burton, Sandra. "A Muddle-Through Mode." *Time,* July 16, 1990.

Cahill, Mary Jane. *Places and Peoples of the World: Israel.* New York: Chelsea House, 1988.

"Chamorro, Violeta (Barrios de)." *Current Biography.* New York: H. W. Wilson, 1990.

Chamorro, Violeta. *Dreams of the Heart: The Autobiography of President Violeta Barrios de Chamorro of Nicaragua.* New York: Simon & Schuster, 1996.

Charlton, Linda. "Indira Gandhi, Born to Politics, Left Her Own Imprint on India." *New York Times,* November 1, 1984.

Christian, Shirley. "Chamorro at Managua Helm: Beloved But Also Under Fire." *New York Times,* April 12, 1991.

———. "Feuds and Killings in Nicaragua Mar Democratic Rule." *New York Times,* February 16, 1993.

Chua-Eoan, Howard G. "All in the Family: Women Leaders in the Third World Owe Their Rise More to Male Dynasties than to Militant Feminism." *Time,* Fall 1990.

Clifton, Tony. "Standing by Her Man." *Newsweek,* November 25, 1996.

"Cresson, Edith." *Current Biography.* New York: H. W. Wilson, 1991.

Crossette, Barbara. "Enthralled by Asia's Ruling Women? Look Again." *New York Times,* November 9, 1996.

Desmond, Edward W. "The Undoing of Benazir." *Time,* January 29, 1990.

Doherty, Katherine M., and Craig A. Doherty. *Benazir Bhutto.* New York: Watts, 1990.

Dorinda Elliott. "The Newest Asian Tiger." *Newsweek,* December 2, 1996.

Dreifus, Claudia. "Real-Life Dynasty: Benazir Bhutto." *New York Times Magazine,* May 15, 1994.

Dyer, Gwynne. "Deadlier than the Male: It's a Trait that Serves Many Women in Power." Minneapolis *Star Tribune,* November 16, 1997.

Fainaru, Steve. "Rightist on way to Victory in Nicaraguan Elections." *Boston Globe,* October 22, 1996.

"Foe of Welfare State to Lead New Zealand." *New York Times,* December 9, 1997.

Foster, Leila Merrell. *Margaret Thatcher: First Woman Prime Minister of Great Britain.* Chicago: Children's Press, 1990.

Friedrich, Otto. "Sad, Lonely, but Never Afraid: Indira Gandhi: 1917-1984." *Time,* November 12, 1984.

Garfinkel, Bernard. *Margaret Thatcher.* New York: Chelsea House, 1985.

Genovese, Michael A., ed. *Women As National Leaders.* Newbury Park, Calif.: Sage Publications, 1993.

Gibbs, Nancy. "Norway's Radical Daughter." *Time*, September 25, 1989.

Golden, Tim. "Nicaraguan Leader Reaffirms Pledge to Oust General." *New York Times*, September 4, 1993.

Great Lives in World Government. New York: Scribner's, 1992.

Greene, Carol. *Indira Nehru Gandhi: Ruler of India.* Chicago: Children's Press, 1985.

Griffiths, John. *Let's Visit Nicaragua.* London: Burke, 1985.

"Here's to You, Mrs. Robinson." *World Press Review*, July 1996.

Hofmann, Paul. "Golda Meir, 80, Dies in Jerusalem; Israelis Acclaim 'Stalwart Lioness.'" *New York Times*, December 9, 1978.

Hole, Dorothy. *Margaret Thatcher: Britain's Prime Minister.* Hillside, N.J.: Enslow, 1990.

Hughes, Libby. *Benazir Bhutto: From Prison to Prime Minister.* Minneapolis: Dillon, 1990.

Indurthy, Rathnam. "Pakistan: Can Democracy Survive?" *USA Today Magazine*, November 1995.

"Irish President Will Not Run Again." *New York Times*, March 13, 1997.

Iyer, Pico. "All in the Family." *Time*, November 12, 1984.

———. "Woman of the Year: President Corazón Aquino." *Time*, January 5, 1987.

Jackson, Guida M. *Women Who Ruled.* Santa Barbara: ABC-CLIO, 1990.

Kamm, Henry. "Karachi Journal: With Blood Tie Sundered, Blood Divides Bhuttos." *New York Times*, January 12, 1994.

Karnow, Stanley. "Cory Aquino's Downhill Slide." *New York Times Magazine*, August 19, 1990.

Keller, Mollie. *Golda Meir.* New York: Franklin Watts, 1983.

Komisar, Lucy. *Corazón Aquino: The Story of a Revolution.* New York: Braziller, 1987.

Kott, Jennifer. *Nicaragua.* New York: Marshall Cavendish, 1995.

"Kumaratunga, Chandrika Bandaranaike." *Current Biography.* New York: H. W. Wilson, 1996.

Light, Julie. "Nicaragua: Autonomous Feminism." *Ms.*, July/August 1991.

Liswood, Laura. "'Madame President.'" *Boston Sunday Globe*, February 15, 1998.

———. *Women World Leaders: Fifteen Great Politicians Tell Their Stories.* London: Pandora, 1995.

Liu, Melinda, and Peter McKillop. "A Habit of Dependency." *Newsweek*, May 11, 1992.

MacFarquhar, Emily. "Bhutto's uphill battle." *U.S. News & World Report*, November 1, 1993.

"Madame 19% Flunks Out." *Time*, April 13, 1992.

Malhotra, Inder. *Indira Gandhi: A Personal and Political Biography*. Boston: Northeastern University Press, 1991.

Nadel, Laurie. *Corazón Aquino: A Journey to Power*. New York: Simon & Schuster, 1987.

Nelan, Bruce W., and William Mader. "A Legacy of Revolution." *Time*, December 3, 1990.

Nelson, Barbara J., and Najma Chowdhury. *Women and Politics Worldwide*. New Haven, Conn.: Yale University Press, 1994.

Newberg, Paula R. "The Two Benazir Bhuttos." *New York Times*, February 11, 1995.

"Nicaragua Security Aide Out; Leader of Army is to be Next." *New York Times*, September 3, 1993.

"Nicaragua's Feuding Parties Strike Deal to End a Standoff." *New York Times*, October 9, 1993.

"Norway Premier Quits, Dismisses Talk of UN Job." *Boston Globe*, October 24, 1996.

"Now the Hard Part: Governing." *Time*. December 12, 1988.

O'Neill, Lois Decker, ed. *The Women's Book of World Records and Achievements*. Garden City, N.Y.: Anchor Press/Doubleday, 1979.

Painton, Frederick. " 'It Is Time to Go.' " *Time*, December 3, 1990.

Parliamentary Group of the Labour Party, Norway. Correspondence to author, February 12, 1997.

Petty, Jill. "Only 5 of 190 World Leaders Are Women. How Are They Doing?" *Ms.*, March/April 1996.

"Philippines Picks Its Future, The." *Economist*, May 16, 1992.

"Post Brundtland." *Economist*, October 26, 1996.

Prokesch, Steven. "Thatcherism: Viable Still?" *New York Times*, November 24, 1990.

Raines, Howell. "Thatcher's Capitalist Revolution." *New York Times Magazine*, May 31, 1987.

Riding, Alan. "Norwegians Signal Doubts on Europe." *New York Times*, February 14, 1993.

Roberts, Cokie, and Steve Roberts. "Mothers' Day in Congress." *USA Weekend*, May 9-11, 1997.

Robinson, Gail. "Power Outage." *World Press Review*, June 1993.

Rohter, Larry. "Nicaragua's New President Changes Pace." *New York Times*, reprinted in *Sun-Sentinel*, February 23, 1997.

Rosca, Ninotchka. "Between the Gun and the Crucifix: Cory Aquino and the Women of the Philippines." *Ms.*, October 1986.

Rosenthal, A. M. "Father and Daughter: A Remembrance." *New York Times*, November 1, 1984.

———. "Indira Gandhi, Slain, Is Succeeded by Son." *New York Times*, November 1, 1984.

Sanger, David E. "Her Term about to End, Aquino Hasn't Made Much Difference to the Poor." *New York Times*, June 8, 1992.

Sapiro, Virginia. *The Political Integration of Women: Roles, Socialization, and Politics*. Urbana, Ill.: University of Illinois Press, 1983.

Schmidt, William E. "Who's in Charge Here? Chances Are It's a Woman." *New York Times*, May 22, 1991.

Schmittroth, Linda, and Mary Reilly McCall. *Women's Almanac*. Detroit: Gale Research, 1997.

Seager, Joni. *The State of Women in the World Atlas*. New York: Penguin, 1997.

Serrill, Michael S. "An Experiment in Woman Power." *Time*, October 6, 1986.

Shenon, Philip. "One Aquino's Painful Stand on Bases." *New York Times*, September 13, 1991.

"Sikh Killers—Cutting Edge of Religious Anger." *U.S. News & World Report*, November 12, 1984.

Sindayen, Nelly, and William Stewart. "Woman of the Year: A Christmas Conversation." *Time*, January 5, 1987.

Slater, Robert. *Golda: The Uncrowned Queen of Israel*. New York: Jonathan David, 1981.

Smith, William E. "Death in the Garden." *Time*, November 12, 1984.

Smolowe, Jill. "A Country Held Hostage." *Time*, September 6, 1993.

———. "After the Revolution." *Time*, March 12, 1990.

Spaeth, Anthony. "When the Barbarians Overrun the Streets." *Time*, March 20, 1995.

"Sri Lanka Ruling Party Wins at Polls." *Boston Globe*, March 23, 1997.

Stevens, William K. "Premier of India Slain by Gunmen." *New York Times*, October 31, 1984.

Stewart, William. "The Next Generation." *Time*, June 3, 1991.

Stuckless, Noreen. "Two Women Who Made it to the Top: Gro Harlem Brundtland, P.M. of Norway and Vigdís Finnbogadóttir, President of Iceland." *Canadian Woman Studies*, Summer 1988.

Thatcher, Margaret. *The Downing Street Years*. New York: HarperCollins, 1993.

————. *The Path to Power*. New York: HarperCollins, 1995.

"Thunder on the Right." *Time*. September 30, 1991.

Tofting, Marina. "Norway: The Price We Pay." *Ms.*, January/February 1991.

Tope, Lily Rose R. *Philippines*. New York: Marshall Cavendish, 1991.

Troyer, Warner, foreword by Gro Harlem Brundtland. *Preserving Our World: A Consumer's Guide to the Brundtland Report*. Toronto: Warglen International Communications, 1990.

Uglow, Jennifer S., ed. *International Dictionary of Women's Biography*. New York, Continuum, 1989.

Uhlig, Mark A. "Chamorro Takes Nicaragua Helm; Hails a New Era." *New York Times*, April 26, 1990.

————. "Opposing Ortega." *New York Times Magazine*, February 11, 1990.

"Violeta Alone." *Economist*, September 11, 1993.

"Voters Reject Joining European Union." *Facts on File*. December 1, 1984.

Whitney, Craig R. "After a Decade of Thatcher, Are Her Ideals Now Britain's?" *New York Times*, May 21, 1989.

————. "Norway Is Planning to Resume Whaling Despite World Ban." *New York Times*, June 30, 1992.

Who's Who of Women in World Politics. "Statistical Survey of Women in World Politics." London: Bowker-Saur, 1991.

Willcoxen, Harriett. *First Lady of India: The Story of Indira Gandhi*. Garden City, N.Y.: Doubleday, 1969.

Wolpert, Stanley. "History's Hold on Pakistan." *New York Times*, November 12, 1996.

"Women and Children First." *Economist*, October 29, 1994.

"Women Left, Right and Centre." *Economist*, March 23, 1991.

"World News: Pakistanis Hail Election Victories." *Boston Globe*, February 16, 1997.

Zubrzycki, John. "Corruption Probe." *World Press Review*, December 1996.

Index

ABOUT THE AUTHOR

JOAN AXELROD-CONTRADA is a freelance writer whose work has appeared in the *Boston Globe* and various other publications. She lives in western Massachusetts with her husband and two children.

Photo Credits